A Crash Course
in Composition

A Crash Course in Composition

Fourth Edition

Elizabeth McMahan
Illinois State University

McGraw-Hill Book Company

New York St. Louis San Francisco Auckland Bogotá Caracas
Colorado Springs Hamburg Lisbon London Madrid Mexico Milan
Montreal New Delhi Oklahoma City Panama Paris San Juan
São Paulo Singapore Sydney Tokyo Toronto

A CRASH COURSE IN COMPOSITION

1 2 3 4 5 6 7 8 9 0 FGR FGR 8 9 3 2 1 0 9 8

ISBN 0-07-045478-7

This book was set in Times Roman by Automated Composition Service, Inc.
The editors were Susan Hurtt, Judith R. Cornwell, and James R. Belser;
the production supervisor was Salvador Gonzales.
The cover was designed by John Hite.
Arcata Graphics/Fairfield was printer and binder.

Acknowledgments appear on pages 271–272
and on this page by reference.

Library of Congress Cataloging-in-Publication Data

McMahan, Elizabeth.
    A crash course in composition.
    Includes index.
    1. English language—Rhetoric.   I. Title.
PE1408.M3323   1989   808'.042   88-13261
ISBN 0-07-045478-7

About the Author

Elizabeth McMahan grew up in College Station, home of the "Fightin' Texas Aggies," where her father taught physics at Texas A & M University. Her BA and MA degrees in English are from the University of Houston; her PhD (in American literature) is from the University of Oregon, where she enjoyed the benefits of a National Defense Education Act Fellowship. She is presently Professor of English and Director of Writing Programs at Illinois State University.

While still in graduate school, McMahan completed the first edition of *A Crash Course in Composition*. Since then, she has embraced the joys of collaborative writing with Susan Day. These two have composed *The Writer's Rhetoric and Handbook*, *The Writer's Handbook*, and *The Writer's Resource: Essays for Composition*, all published by McGraw-Hill. With another firm and with a third collaborator, Robert Funk, they have produced *Literature and the Writing Process*, *Keeping in Touch: Writing Clearly* (a basic writing text), and *The Elements of Writing about Literature and Film*.

McMahan considers herself most fortunate in having a husband who is a feminist; four cats (one crazy); two fat, white geese; one beige, rotund corgi; and a house on Lake Bloomington where she composes on an IBM PC.

To my dear Aunt Helen,
with love and admiration.

Contents

2

FURTHER ADVICE FOR THOSE WHO NEED IT

Theme-Grading Guide

Preface

The purpose of this revision of *A Crash Course in Composition* remains the same as in previous editions: to provide, in a conversational tone that is pleasant to read and easy to understand, concise instruction about writing. This text is designed for people who want help in learning how to organize ideas, develop paragraphs, craft sentences, and insert punctuation; who want to know what is acceptable and what is not in standard English; and who want to acquire all this information as quickly and painlessly as possible.

As with each previous edition, I have struggled against the temptation to add too much. Of course, I have updated the "Glossary of Usage," fine-tuned the prose throughout, and added bits and pieces of advice here and there. Noteworthy additions are these: further instruction about audience and purpose, about choosing words precisely, and about using the passive voice effectively. Although I strongly favor active voice, I have become reconciled to the fact that many writers, especially student writers taking courses in education, criminology, and the social and the hard sciences, are often required to use the passive voice; thus they need to learn to do it well.

Because I believe that organizing before writing provides the most efficient and effective means of composing, I have emphasized the planning stage of the process by giving it a separate chapter. And because I believe that precise word choice is essential in good writing, I have given a separate chapter to diction. These two changes produced the added benefit of shortening all the chapters in Part One—the only section that needs to be thoroughly read, not simply consulted.

This edition includes, of course, the new, streamlined Modern Language Association (MLA) documentation style and provides a fresh sample student research paper illustrating its use. Complete instructions for using the increasingly popular APA (American Psychological Association) documentation style has also been added. Those who still cherish the old MLA style will find brief instruction remaining for its use.

My sincere thanks to the people who have assisted me with this revision: my astute reviewers—Denny Berthiaume, Foothills College; Harvey Birenbaum, San Jose State University; Sister Mary Faulkner, College of St. Benedict; Mary Gilliland, Cornell University; Jon Jellema, Grand Valley State College; Carolyn Russell, Rio Hondo College, and Joel Zienty, Lake Michigan College; my literate helpmate—Dan LeSeure, my good friend—Michele Finley; my invaluable editors—Emily Barrosse, Judith Cornwell, Sue Hurtt, and James Belser, and their efficient assistants—Kathleen Francisco, Christina Cenkner, and Pat Pfaus. I am, as usual, especially grateful to my colleague Susie Day who supplied many interesting writing ideas and several of the wittier entries in this text.

Elizabeth McMahan

A Crash Course
in Composition

Part One

How to Put a Paper Together

Chapter 1

Ponder Your Approach

Writing well involves hard work. There's no sense in pretending otherwise. But as my colleague Charlie Harris says, "I hate to write, but I love to have written." That's it, exactly. Writing is challenging but rewarding—if you do a good job. And if you're not going to do a good job, you might as well not do it at all.

WHY BOTHER?

The rewards are more than psychological. Writing skillfully is one of the most useful crafts you can develop—essential even—and valuable to prospective employers. You will greatly improve your chances of landing a good job if you can write clear, correct expository prose. That's the kind of writing dealt with in this book: not poetry or drama or fiction, but informative writing. If you'd like to consider a more immediate need, there's no honest way to get through college without being able to write. You simply can't hope to get into law or medical school without a thorough knowledge of *standard English*—the language spoken and written by educated people in this country. Whether you're planning to enter engineering, teaching, social work, or any business or professional career, you'll have to write: memos, letters, reports, instructions, lesson plans, summaries, case files.

Let's face it. You need to be able to write. This book can help you learn to write well. I've tried to make the process as painless as possible, but writing is seldom easy. It requires precision. It requires thinking. I struggle and sigh and squint and swear; I chew my nails, twiddle my thumbs, furrow my brow, gnash my teeth—but eventually I write. And you can, too, if you're willing to work at it.

CLARITY IS THE KEYNOTE

The important thing to get straight in the beginning is this: You want your readers to *understand what you write*. No need for suspense. No call for ambiguity. Let your readers know at the outset what you're going to discuss and then discuss it. Graceful phrasing and a rich vocabulary are welcome stylistic adornments, but compared with the necessity for *total clarity*, they are secondary. Such refinements can wait until the polishing process—the revising that every good writer feels compelled to do after completing a first draft.

THINK BEFORE YOU WRITE

As you begin to plan your paper, you need to consider three things:

1 Your purpose: Why am I writing?
2 Your audience: Who am I writing for?
3 Your thesis: What am I going to write about?

These questions are equally important, and your answer to one will often affect your response to the others. For purposes of discussion, let's consider them one by one.

DECIDING YOUR PURPOSE

Before you start writing, you need to ask yourself what your purpose is. Why are you exerting all this energy and straining your brain to do this piece of writing? It may be an honest answer to say because your teacher or your boss told you to, but it's not a useful answer. Think beyond that immediate response to the reason that makes writing worthwhile. What do you hope to accomplish? Are you writing *to inform* your readers? Do you hope *to persuade* your readers to change their minds about some issue? Perhaps you simply want to *entertain* them. Or you may be keeping a journal or a diary just for your own uses, with no need to consider any other readers than yourself.

Your purpose affects your whole approach to writing: how you begin, whether you state or imply your thesis, what specific details you choose, how you organize the material, how you conclude, as well as what words you select for each sentence. You should give thought to your purpose before you start even the preliminary planning stage.

CONSIDERING YOUR AUDIENCE

You can't successfully determine why you're writing without also considering this question: Who is going to read what you write? Your audience may be a single person—your boss, perhaps, your history professor, your senator. Or you may sometimes wish to reach a larger audience—your city council, your composition class, the readership of some publication like your campus or city newspaper, *Time* magazine, or *Rolling Stone*.

If your purpose, for instance, is to inform, you need to think about how to present your information to your specific audience most effectively. You can see at once that the larger your audience, the more touchy the problem. If you're writing a letter to the editor of your local newspaper explaining the appeal of reggae music, you'll be addressing people of all ages with assorted dispositions and prejudices. You need to choose your words carefully and present your information calmly— or you may end up with next to no readers at all.

If, however, you're writing a letter to the editor of *Rolling Stone*, your verbal tactics would need to be different. Since your audience here would be primarily people who know a lot about popular music, you should omit background information explaining how reggae originated. You would write in a more conversational manner, using current slang and even music jargon, since your audience could be expected to understand the jargon and not be put off by the slang.

Audience Analysis Checklist

In order to increase your abilities in evaluating your audience, ask yourself the following questions during the process of planning your paper.

1 How much will my readers already know about my topic?
2 Will they respond emotionally to my topic? Will I need to be especially careful not to offend them? If so, how?
3 Will they be interested in my topic? Perhaps bored by it? If they may be bored, how can I get them interested?
4 Will they be in agreement with me? Opposed? Neutral?
5 How well educated in general are my readers?
6 Do they fall into any particular age group?
7 Is it important to consider their race, sex, marital status, possible parenthood, or religion?
8 Do they identify with any political groups (like Republicans, Democrats, libertarians, socialists)?
9 Are they members of any public interest group (Moral Majority, Common Cause, National Organization for Women, American Civil Liberties Union, Sierra Club, etc.)?
10 How do they make their living? Are they rich, poor, middle-class?

Temper Your Tone

Although on occasion you may want to make your audience angry about something—injustice, poverty, bigotry—you always want to avoid making them angry at you. Your purpose in writing is to persuade them to agree with you. Therefore, try to adopt a tone that won't antagonize your readers.

Tone means the attitude of the writer toward what is being written. Tone can be gentle, sad, strident, angry, serious, sympathetic, supercilious, humorous, playful, poignant, admiring, earnest, curt, sarcastic, ironic, sardonic, or neutral. Since tone always depends to some extent upon how the words are received by the readers, be careful if you decide to adopt an ironic or sarcastic tone. You could easily be misunderstood. Remember that the tone of your voice does not carry over to the written word. A neutral tone may be the best tone for most writing. Before you write, consider your purpose and choose a tone that seems appropriate.

You may sometimes *want* to write abusively when you feel

abused, but try to resist the temptation. You'll only turn your readers off. Mark Twain never published a line or even mailed a letter until his gentle wife Olivia had cleared his prose. You can begin to see why if you'll read his famous letter to the gas company.

Hartford, February 12, 1891

Dear Sirs:

Some day you will move me almost to the verge of irritation by your chuckle-headed (expletive deleted) fashion of shutting your (expletive deleted) gas off without giving any notice to your (expletive deleted) parishioners. Several times you have come within an ace of smothering half of this household in their beds and blowing up the other half by this idiotic, not to say criminal, custom of yours. And it has happened again to-day. Haven't you a telephone?

Ys

S L Clemens

Needless to say, Livy didn't let that one pass. Twain revised his correspondence daily as his rage subsided, until he produced a temperate version that wouldn't invite a libel suit. Try to do the same with your own writing. Adopt a tone that will allow you to be convincing but not offensive.

ANALYZING THE EFFECTS OF AUDIENCE AND PURPOSE

Think carefully about both purpose and audience as you plan your paper. Continue to keep them in mind as you write. Consider them again as you revise. These overlapping concepts are crucial, for they affect your tone and your tactics.

Notice, for instance, the extensive changes that occur in the following three short passages as I write every one on the same topic (the lack of vegetarian fare in the Snack Shop) but change the purpose each time. The audience here is the Director of Food Services in the Student Union.

1. Purpose: To Inform

Although the food served in the Snack Shop of the Union is appetizing and economical, the menu offers only a single entree suitable for a vegetarian—a grilled cheese sandwich. An expanded menu would better serve the needs of all students.

2. Purpose: To Entertain

Even a toasty, golden-brown grilled cheese sandwich becomes a loathsome thing if the hungry person is trying to choke one down for the twenty-seventh day in a row. Our friends munch contentedly on a whole array of sandwiches—hamburgers, reubens, ham and turkey combinations, hot pastrami—while we vegetarians chew sullenly on our same old grilled cheese.

3. Purpose: To Persuade

While the food served in the Snack Shop of our Union is appetizing and economical, the menu offers little variety for vegetarians. Besides your tasty grilled cheese sandwich, could you perhaps also offer egg salad or fried egg sandwiches? We would especially appreciate your adding a salad bar, which should prove popular with many of your patrons and thus profitable for you as well.

Note what happens in the next three examples when the topic remains the same but the *audience* changes. This time I will address my fellow vegetarians in a letter in the student newspaper.

4. Purpose: To Inform

Every day we eat lunch in the Snack Shop of the Union because it's the closest and the cheapest place. And every day we end up ordering the same thing—a grilled cheese sandwich—because that's the only vegetarian item on the menu. We're astonished that at a university the size of ours the food service takes no account of vegetarians' preferences.

5. Purpose: To Entertain

When we trudge over to the Snack Shop for lunch—exhausted from our morning classes, perishing for some wholesome food—

we're confronted by a menu offering nothing but a disgusting array of dead animals: dead cow on a bun, dead pig on rye, dead fowl on a roll. We starving vegetarians must make do with a barely edible slice of imitation cheese grilled between two pale pieces of greasy balloon bread. We could get a more nutritious and tasty meal by munching grass out on the quad.

6. Purpose: To Persuade

Vegetarians, unite! Our reasonable requests have so far produced no changes in the meat-laden menu at the Union Snack Shop. In order to convince the food service people that a substantial number of vegetarians are potential customers, we need to state our appeal collectively. Stop by the Food Services office next time you're in the Union and tell the manager that we need a salad bar.

Discussion Exercise 1-1

1 In the first group of examples, addressed to the Director of Food Services, what details change when the purpose becomes to entertain rather than to inform? Can you tell why? What differences do you notice in word choice? Do you find them appropriate? Why?

2 What different details do you find in the third passage? Why are they introduced? Why do you think the terms *appetizing*, *economical*, and *tasty* appear?

3 In the second group of passages, addressed to fellow vegetarians, the words chosen to describe the meat sandwiches in example 5 are quite different from those used in example 2. Can you explain why?

4 Consider the descriptions of the grilled cheese sandwich in examples 2 and 5. Can you account for the differences? Would a nonvegetarian find example 5 amusing, do you think? If not, why?

5 If you examine all six passages, you will notice that the most pronounced changes occur when the purpose becomes to entertain. What significant difference can you observe when you compare the passages aimed to inform (1 and 4) with those designed to persuade (3 and 6)?

Writing Exercise   **1-2**

Choose either of the following topics.

1   Write a letter to the School Board of your former high school suggesting
    that too much (or too little) emphasis is being given to the Latin Club, to
    the vocational program, to the cheerleading squad, to the baseball team,
    or to counseling students.

    Then rewrite the letter to address the President of the Student Council.
    Try to convince that person to rouse the student body to action on your
    issue.

    Your purpose in both letters will be to persuade, but remember that a
    humorous approach can sometimes be the most persuasive—depending upon
    the topic and the audience.

    If you don't know the correct form for writing a business letter, follow
    the format used in the sample job application letter in Appendix B.

2   Write a brief account of Moses parting the Red Sea and marching his people
    across. First write a version to present at the Wednesday Night Bible Study
    Group. Then write a version to appear as a news story in *Time* magazine.
    Your purpose in both is to inform. If you don't remember the biblical story,
    choose some historical event, like the assassination of President Lincoln,
    and write a version first for the grade school publication *The Weekly Reader*;
    then write another account for *Time* magazine.

FINDING A THESIS

One of the early decisions in the process of writing involves choosing
(or being assigned) a subject of some sort to write about. In composition class you may be allowed to choose your topic. In history class
you are more likely to be told the topic. On the job you will probably
be required to report in writing on an assigned subject. After you have
chosen or been assigned a topic, you need to find an approach that
allows you to cover the subject within your word limit. Eventually,
you should be able to write out this main idea in a single sentence—
your *thesis statement*.

Once you have worked it out, your thesis should clearly state the
point you want to make about your subject. If, for instance, your topic

is conservation, you need to narrow it considerably for a three-page paper. You might decide to write just about protecting wildlife. But even that is too broad an idea to cover in a brief essay. You could then limit yourself to seals. But now, ask yourself, what *about* seals? What is the point you want to make? You could assert that seals should be protected from industry by international treaty. Or you could argue that people should not buy any product made of sealskin in order to keep industry from finding the slaughter profitable.

REMEMBER: **Your thesis should contain a verb to say something about your subject.**

Topic:	Drugs
Topic:	Drug abuse
Workable thesis:	Drug abuse can occur with perfectly legal prescription drugs.
Workable thesis:	Excessive use of alcohol constitutes the number 1 drug abuse problem in the United States.

A good thesis should make your readers want to read further in order to find out what you have to say about this interesting idea. Be sure the idea is indeed interesting, not a trite or simple-minded idea like "Sports build character" or "Motherhood is a joyful experience that no woman should miss." The writer of that last sentence hadn't thought about the idea. Is motherhood joyful for a poor woman with no husband and nine children? Are women's personalities so similar that such a generalization could be true? We all find ourselves writing down unexamined ideas once in a while. A thoughtful rereading of whatever you write can help you avoid making this weakness public.

Discussion Exercise   **1-3**

Some of the sentences below are workable thesis statements for an essay of about 500 words, but some need to be made more specific. Pick out the successful ones, and indicate what's wrong with the others.

See if you can make every one into a reasonably good thesis. But first, here are five workable thesis statements to inspire you.

A Many Americans spend so much time in front of the TV set that they never really experience their own lives. (In the introduction of your paper, this thesis might appear in a livelier form, like "Turn off the TV and turn on to life!")

B I think that college students and teachers would be happier with education if people didn't enroll in college before the age of 25.

C On a sunny summer morning last year, I realized that I was ultimately alone.

D The perfect omelet is fluffy, light, delicately browned, and even attainable if the cook follows five practical guidelines.

E In Shakespeare's *Hamlet*, Ophelia's insanity and suicide represent what would have happened to Hamlet had he been female.

Now try to whip these into shape:

  1 Television commercials are an outrage.
  2 Freedom and independence carry with them responsibilities and consequences.
  3 I'm going to describe the dying flowers and yellowing leaves outside my window.
  4 My dog and my boyfriend are much alike.
  5 I learned not to worry when I was 16.
  6 Thousands of Americans go through the vicious cycle of eating until they are overweight and then dieting until they reduce.
  7 People's views on capital punishment are very controversial.
  8 The purpose of of this paper is to compare and contrast the Catholic schools and the public schools.
  9 Do you feel cheated because you can't grow a beard?
  10 Making a lemon pie is easy.

MUDDLING MAY BE PART OF THE PROCESS

As you are working on your thesis and thinking about audience and purpose, you will probably also be dredging up ideas to use in the paper, a task I have not yet touched on. The writing process is too involved, too recursive, to be described as a neat and orderly progression. But since my writing in this textbook must be neat and orderly to be easily understood, you can see the problem. I can scarcely avoid explaining the process one part at a time. So, let me make clear that these parts can often overlap, can occur simultaneously, or can even sometimes be done in reverse order (as, for example, when you write your introduction after finishing your paper).

If you are a dedicated writer, you will likely spend a lot of time mucking about—scratching out words, tossing out paragraphs, squeezing sentences between the lines, scribbling new ideas on your outline, drawing arrows to insertions, gazing into space as you search for the right word or the perfect example, and sometimes throwing it all in the wastebasket and starting over.

A FEW WORDS ABOUT WORD PROCESSORS

Since writing well is such a messy process, a writer's best friend is not diamonds or a dog but a word processor. If you can lay hands on one, by all means do so. It won't by itself make a better writer of you, but it will enable you to become a better writer with greater ease. Here are some of its advantages.

1 You don't have to worry about any kind of errors as you compose because they can be corrected with no muss, no fuss, no bother.
2 You can erase with the touch of a key.
3 You can insert words or move them around wherever you want them (even whole paragraphs) with astonishing ease.
4 You can use a spelling checker to tell you which words you have spelled too creatively. It will catch your typos, too—except when you have typed the wrong word (like *their* for *there*, *car* for *cat*); so you must still proofread.
5 You can turn out perfect copy, even though (like me) you're a hopelessly incompetent typist.

Programs are available that will even help you with revision by analyzing your writing and then telling you if you're using the passive voice too much, if you've made an error in grammar, or if you're using too many multisyllable words. But whether you have access to one of these magical programs or not, you should start processing your words if possible. You'll find it's easier than putting pen to paper. It's more efficient. And it's more fun.

Chapter 2

Produce a Plausible Plan

In my opinion, the most efficient method of writing involves thinking about what to say and how to say it before beginning to compose. What major points will you present? In what order? What specific details will you include? To structure all this information, you need a plan of some sort.

You don't necessarily need a tidy, formal outline, complete with roman numerals and A, B, C headings like the ones in this chapter. But you should at least get down on paper the main ideas you intend to present and figure out the order in which you will take them up. You can, if you're eager to get started, think up your supporting evidence as you go. Or you can supply missing examples and illustrations as you revise your first draft. Your scratch outline is a flexible guide. You can rearrange points, add ideas, or leave out portions if you discover a better arrangement as you write.

START BY BRAINSTORMING

As you're working out a thesis, jot down every idea that comes to mind pertaining to your subject. After you've come up with a workable thesis, continue searching your mind (and maybe a few magazine articles or books) for more information. Consult your friends, also, to see whether they have any ideas or further knowledge on the matter. Write down every notion, whether it seems exactly to the point or not. You can easily scratch out things you don't need, and you may end up altering your thesis slightly to suit the available facts.

Let's assume that in horticulture class you have been assigned a 500-word paper on home gardening. Since you're not interested in growing flowers, you narrow the topic at once to home vegetable gardening. That's still a subject more suited to a book than a short essay. How about organic vegetable gardening? Better, but 500 words isn't much—only three or four well-developed paragraphs, plus a brief introduction and conclusion. You need to narrow the topic some more. How about fighting bugs organically? That sounds promising.

Now, what *about* fighting bugs organically? "Fighting bugs organically allows home gardeners to avoid the dangers of pesticides." There you have a good preliminary thesis. What supporting evidence can you think of that might prove useful in such an essay? If you think awhile, you may end up with a jumbled list something like this:

Some insects eat garden pests.
Soapy water kills some insects but not hardy plants.
Strong garlic water discourages some pests.
Slugs like beer—and will drown themselves in it, given the chance.
Useful insects can be purchased by mail order.
Praying mantises like to eat caterpillars and mites.
Ladybugs zap aphids.
Milky spore disease kills Japanese beetles.
Cabbage worms are zonked by *Bacillus thuringiensis*.
Pick off insects by hand (drown or suffocate them in a jar).
Birds eat insects.
Laying aluminum foil on the ground will drive aphids to suicide.
Green lacewings eat mealybugs like crazy.

BRINGING ORDER OUT OF CHAOS

You now need three or four main ideas—in this case, methods of controlling insect pests—to serve as the major points in your outline. Keep looking over your list to see if you can discover patterns. Try to determine which are major ideas, which are supporting details.

Note that "Some insects eat garden pests" is a major idea. You have several examples to support it. Perhaps you'll want to rephrase the idea for greater clarity: "Bring in natural enemies to kill pests." As supporting evidence, you can mention praying mantises, ladybugs, and green lacewings (plus the specific insects they control) and note that these useful insects can be purchased by mail. That's plenty for one paragraph.

You may detect several supporting details that are similar and only need to have a major heading added. Notice in your list that these items all share a common trait:

> Putting out beer for slugs
> Laying down aluminum foil to entrap aphids
> Squirting soapy water or garlic water on plants

These methods all use products found usually in the kitchen. You could group these three under the heading, "Try safe and easy household remedies."

Two other items on the list clearly belong together: milky spore disease and *Bacillus thuringiensis*. (You discover such unusual remedies through research—in this case, by reading Lawrence Sheehan's "Garden Club Notes: Fighting Bugs Organically," in *Harper's*, April 1979, which served as a model for this sample outline.) Since these techniques work by introducing diseases fatal to insects but harmless to plants and people, you could head this section, "Introduce insect diseases to destroy pests."

Only two items in the brainstorming list remain unused: picking insects off by hand and encouraging birds to come to your garden. Probably picking bugs off by hand is too tiresome to be a practical suggestion. And enticing birds may hurt more than help. Birds eat bugs indiscriminately—the ladybugs along with the aphids—and are exceptionally fond of many succulent garden vegetables as well. You'd better let those leftover ideas go, unless you decide to mention in your conclusion that if all else fails, the dedicated gardener can always pick off the beastly bugs one by one.

ARRANGING YOUR POINTS   *9/12/90*

After you've chosen the main ideas and supporting details, the last step involves deciding in what order to present your ideas. Since there's no chronology (time order) involved in this particular plan, begin with a fairly strong and interesting point to get your readers' attention. End with your strongest point to leave the readers feeling that you've said something worthwhile. With this pest-control outline, you could almost flip a coin. But since the household remedies are the cheapest and most entertaining to describe, you might well begin there. Save the section on importing natural enemies for the end, since it sounds like a dramatic and effective solution.

SAMPLE OUTLINE

Your outline, then, will look something like this, if you take time to make it look neat:

THESIS: **Fighting bugs organically allows home gardeners to avoid the dangers of pesticides.**

Introduction
  I   Try safe and easy household remedies.
      A   Set out trays of beer to attract slugs, which drown in it.
      B   Spray soapy water (not detergent) or garlic water on plants.
      C   Spread aluminum foil under plants to disorient aphids, thus luring them to their doom.
 II   Introduce insect diseases to destroy pests.
      A   Milky spore disease kills larvae of Japanese beetles.
      B   *Bacillus thuringiensis* sprayed on soil is deadly to cabbage worms.
      C   Both remedies are available at garden stores.

III Bring in natural enemies to fight pests.
    A Praying mantises devour caterpillars and mites.
    B Ladybugs consume quantities of aphids.
    C Green lacewings feed on mealybugs.
    D These useful insects can be ordered by mail.
Conclusion

In the essay from which this outline was adapted, Lawrence Sheehan uses these more imaginative (but less informative) headings for his main points:

  I Hand-to-hand combat   (for "Household remedies")
 II Biological warfare   (for "Insect diseases")
III Hired-guns approach   (for "Natural enemies")

In writing your paper, you may want to employ such colorful language, but in the planning stage, clarity is more important. In the outline set your ideas down in a clear and orderly fashion. Then, when you revise your first draft of the paper, you can make the phrasing witty and entertaining. Remember, though: *Clarity is the keynote.*

Exercise   **2-1**

The following outline illustrates a number of weaknesses: supporting points that don't really support, minor points that pose as major points, major points that lack supporting evidence, etc. Study this sorry example until you have located all its shortcomings; then revise the whole by adding, omitting, and rearranging as necessary to produce a tidy outline.

THESIS: **Studying in a dorm is impossible for anyone who lacks unswerving discipline.**

  I Phones ringing and stereos playing keep me from concentrating.
 II Friends drop in and keep me from studying.
    A Card playing and bull sessions interrupt me.
    B Watching TV is more fun than studying.

III Neighbors are forever partying.
   A Loud music, talking, and laughing disturb me.
IV Studying is really hard for me.
   A I fall asleep.
   B Chemistry 101 is beyond me.

CHECK YOUR PLAN FOR UNITY

Unity is something we never require of casual conversation: it's fine if you wander a little off the track and tell about the Bluebird Saloon in Denver in the middle of a discussion about Humphrey Bogart films.

But in an expository essay, unity is important: you must not go on about the Bluebird in the middle of an *essay* about Bogart films, even though you had a beer there after seeing *The Maltese Falcon* at a nearby theater. Such a departure from the main subject is called a *digression*. A paragraph or essay has unity if it sticks to the main point. It lacks unity if it wanders across the street for a drink.

Since the unity and coherence of your paper depend largely on the way you order your ideas—that is, on your plan or outline—you should take a few minutes to go over it after you finish it. Check these points carefully:

1 Make sure every major heading or idea relates to your thesis.
2 Make sure every major heading has adequate supporting details.
3 Make sure every supporting detail relates to its major heading.
4 Don't let any major point get buried as a supporting detail or any minor points get elevated as major headings.
5 Don't allow any careless repetition of ideas anywhere.

If you will take the trouble to unify your outline this way, you can't possibly end up with slipshod organization or an essay that wanders away from the topic.

PATTERN YOUR DEVELOPMENT

The sample outline about battling bugs was put together by classification—by sorting out the methods of killing garden pests without using insecticides. While classification is a common method of organizing material, experienced writers employ a number of patterns for ordering and developing their ideas—quite often using several different methods in the same piece.

Practicing these various ways of organizing material is a lot like doing finger exercises when learning to play the piano. Through practice you internalize a skill: you make the execution of that skill second nature so that you can use the techniques without having to think about them consciously. Once you become an expert writer, you'll not need to mull over which patterns to use as you develop your ideas. By then you'll have the various methods stored in your brain, and you'll use them to structure your material without giving the techniques themselves a moment's thought.

Your instructor may perhaps wish to have you practice these patterns by writing paragraphs instead of essays in each mode. You are, of course, more likely to employ these patterns in developing individual paragraphs and passages instead of complete essays.

SPATIAL STRUCTURE

This first method of development, used for description, will seldom form the basis of an entire paper, unless you're writing for practice or for pleasure. But you will probably use description in virtually everything you write—especially if you write interestingly.

Description

Most authorities on writing suggest that you can organize descriptions spatially—top to bottom, left to right, near to far, etc. This is true. You can describe your cat from nose to tail. But where do you include the texture of the fur, the stripes or spots, the color of the paws? And what about the meow? And the various ways the cat moves? Good description involves working a number of details into some spatial arrangement.

First, consider your purpose. Do you want to arouse an emotional response in your readers? Or are you trying to convey a word picture, without emotion but sharp and clear as a photograph? Your choice of words and details will differ according to the effect you want. Before you begin writing, look—really *look*—at what you plan to describe. Maybe you'll want to smell and taste and touch it as well. Then try to record your sense impressions—the exact shapes, the lights and shades, the textures, the tastes, the sounds, the smells. Don't include everything, of course, or you may overwhelm your readers. Carefully select the details that suit your purpose in order to give your audience a sharp impression of what you're describing. Then search for the precise words to convey that picture.

In this choice descriptive paragraph. Mark Twain takes his readers with him through the woods and into a meadow:

> Beyond the road where the snakes sunned themselves was a dense young thicket, and through it a dim-lighted path led a quarter of a mile; then out of the dimness one emerged abruptly upon a level great prairie which was covered with wild strawberry plants, vividly starred with prairie pinks, and walled in on all sides by forests. The strawberries were fragrant and fine and in the season we were generally there in the crisp freshness of the early morning, while the dew-beads still sparkled upon the grass and the woods were ringing with the first song of the birds.

> —Mark Twain's *Autobiography* (1924)

A contemporary master of description is Annie Dillard, who allows us both to see and hear the ocean through her selection of details and choice of words in this brief passage from her article ''Innocence in the Galápagos,'' in *Harper's* magazine (May 1975):

> The white beach was a havoc of lava boulders black as clinkers, sleek with spray, and lambent as brass in the sinking sun. To our left a dozen sea lions were body-surfing in the long green combers that rose, translucent, half a mile offshore. When the combers broke, the shoreline boulders rolled. I could feel the roar in the rough rock on which I sat; I could hear the grate inside each long backsweeping sea, the rumble of a rolled million rocks muffled in splashes and the seethe before the next wave's heave.

Out of thousands of possible details, Dillard chooses a few that are powerful and appeal to our senses. Remember that good descriptive details will enliven almost any kind of writing. Be sure to observe carefully, select telling details, and search for the exact words.

Topics for Descriptive Writing

1 Describe as thoroughly as possible in one sentence how a cat's fur feels, how modeling clay feels, how soft rain feels, how hard rain feels, how a hangover feels. Or describe in a sentence how a snake moves, how a cat walks, how a dog greets you; or how a vampire looks, or a werewolf, or a visitor from outer space.

2 Describe a food you hate or love with as much sensory detail as possible.

3 Choose one brief experience that has sensuous association for you—something like this: A person walks by wearing the same perfume you wore in the eleventh grade, or you pet a dog that looks just exactly like old Spot, your devoted companion all through grade school, or you hear a special "golden oldie" on the radio. Write a descriptive paragraph in which you develop that brief experience.

4 Describe a place (like a classroom, the cafeteria, the coffee shop, the dorm lounge, the Dean's office) and try to convey your attitude toward it through your use of specific details. Avoid making a statement about your feelings.

5 Describe the place in which you feel most at peace—or most ill at ease. Choose details that appeal to the senses.

CHRONOLOGICAL STRUCTURE

Most of the time, writers organize material in two ways: according to chronological sequence or according to logical sequence. Let's take up chronological development first because it's easier.

Narrative Writing

Brief narratives are frequently used in introductions to gain the readers' interest. Narratives are also useful as supporting evidence—to prove a point through an account of a personal experience. Although narratives are seldom appropriate in academic essays or business writing, you will find that telling an entertaining story proves a good way to enliven various other kinds of writing. And sometimes a narrative may prove to be the perfect form for an entire essay, article, or speech.

Since a narrative recounts an event or an experience, you can simply arrange the details in the order in which they happened. Of critical importance, though, is choosing the right details and focusing on the most significant happenings. While narrative is perhaps the easiest kind of writing to do, it is surely one of the hardest to do well. You may find it necessary to fictionalize the details of your experience somewhat in order to keep your readers interested. And you must be especially careful to maintain a consistent point of view.

But take note: In a piece of pure narrative writing, do not state your thesis in your introduction. Put your thesis or purpose on your scratch outline; then leave the main idea implied in the paper itself. You don't want to take the edge off.

You need in all good writing to make a point of some sort, but you want to avoid just tacking on a moral as the conclusion of your narrative. Say you're asked to write a narrative account of some experience you remember from your childhood. Anything you can recall vividly probably has some significance. Be sure to have in mind before you write what that significance is and how you're going to bring it out. If you remember, for instance, one awful day in sixth grade when your gym teacher made you—a 97-pound weakling—wrestle a 150-pound tarzan, you'll want to include the bloodthirsty cries of your classmates and the sadistic chuckles of your gym teacher in order to emphasize the inhumanity of the incident. You don't have to tell your readers the point: if you write it well, they'll see it for themselves.

Topics for Narrative Writing

1 I learned _____ the hard way.
2 Write an account of your initiation into some element of the adult world of which you were unaware as a child: violence, hypocrisy, prejudice, sexuality, etc.
3 Tell about the first time you remember being punished at school (or at home).
4 Tell the story of a tough ethical decision you once had to make and of what happened afterward.
5 Write a narrative to support or deny some familiar proverb, like ''Honesty is the best policy,'' ''Nice guys finish last,'' or ''Home is where the heart is.''

Process Papers

One of the most practical kinds of writing explains a process, i.e., tells readers how to do something or how something works. Often explaining a process provides the material for a complete essay or set of instructions, but you may, on occasion, want to explain a process as a section in a longer piece. An essay focusing on the advantages of organic gardening, for instance, might well include a paragraph explaining how to make compost.

Chronological structure, point by point, is the usual way to organize process writing. Remember to start at the beginning. If you're going to explain how to bathe a large, reluctant dog, you'll want first to suggest putting on old clothes or a bathing suit and proceed from there. Your outline might look something like this:

THESIS: **How to wash a dog without losing your temper or frightening the washee.**

  I   What to wear.
     A   In summer—old clothes or bathing suit.
     B   In winter—next to nothing in the shower.
 II   Gathering the implements.
     A   Mild soap or dog shampoo.
     B   Lots of old towels.
     C   Hand-held hairdryer—if winter.
III   Where to do it.
     A   In summer—on driveway or patio to avoid killing grass with soap.
     B   In winter—in bathtub with shower curtain drawn.
     C   If no shower curtain, wait till summer.
 IV   Reassuring the animal.
     A   Dog thinks you plot a drowning.
     B   Talk continually in comforting tones.
  V   The actual washing.
     A   Wet entire dog, apply soap or shampoo, work up lather.
     B   Keep soap out of eyes and ears.
     C   Don't forget the underside and tail.
     D   Rinse very thoroughly.

VI Drying the dog.
    A Dog will shake—like it or not.
    B Rub damp-dry with towels.
    C If winter, finish with hand-held hairdryer.

You might conclude that having a shiny, fragrant, flealess dog makes all this tribulation worthwhile. Or you might instead conclude that dog owners in their right minds who can afford the fee should pack the beast off to the veterinary clinic and let the experts do it.

A process paper, although easy to organize, is difficult to make interesting. Include as many descriptive words and lively verbs as you can without making the whole thing sound grotesque. You may assume if you're describing a technical process, such as how to clean a carburetor or how to replace a light switch, that probably your readers will follow out of a desire for enlightenment, so there's no obligation to entertain. But instead you must be doubly sure to identify all parts and to explain each and every step.

Identify your audience before you plan. Who are your readers? How much do they already know about the process? How much more do they need to know about it? Instructions for tuning a TV, for instance, will be written entirely differently for the person who owns the set than for the person who repairs it.

Here are some tips for good process writing: (1) Define any unfamiliar terms; (2) be as specific as possible; (3) include reasons for each step; and (4) provide warnings about typical mistakes or hazards.

Some processes do not lend themselves to an easy chronological organization—subjects like "How to choose a suitable marriage partner" or "How to care for a praying mantis." For such topics you must fall back on logical organization, which is covered in the next section.

Topics for Process Writing

1 How to train an animal (dog, parrot, turtle, cat, etc.).
2 How to get rid of a bad habit. Choose only one habit to discuss: nail biting, smoking, interrupting others, or the like.
3 How to build a successful campfire.

4 Find out and describe how some simple, familiar thing works (for example:
   soap, can opener, hand eggbeater, wart remover, ballpoint pen).
5 How to come about on a windsurfer, or how to impress someone by doing
   a stunt on a skateboard.

LOGICAL STRUCTURE

Most of the writing you'll be called upon to do will probably require
organizing according to some sort of logic. For instance, if you're
writing a paper which suggests no special kind of structure, your most
logical approach is probably to arrange your ideas from the least
impressive to the most compelling point. Since your final point remains
foremost in the minds of your readers as they appraise the quality of
your paper, you might as well make it your best idea. Or you might
decide to arrange your concepts from the least complicated to the most
complex. Or you could work from the smallest to the largest, like this:

1 Tolerable bores
2 Agonizing bores
3 Stupefying bores

But finding an organization for more complex material requires thought
and ingenuity. Following are some suggestions that you may find
helpful in various writing situations.

Classification and Analysis

When you *classify*, you take many items and sort them out into a few
groups. When you *analyze*, you take one item and divide it into its
component parts. Say your subject is squashes. If you outline "Three
Types of Edible Squash," you're classifying; if you outline "Three
Parts of a Squash Blossom," you're analyzing. Both processes are
based on logical division, and both require the same kind of organizational pattern.

We classify and analyze things all the time with no struggle at all.
We classify political candidates into Republican, Democrat, Populist,
or Socialist; we classify doughnuts into plain, glazed, chocolate-
covered, and jelly-filled. We analyze whenever we reveal and explain

the parts of something. Solving a problem, explaining a process, arguing a point, speculating on cause and effect, interpreting literature—all involve analysis.

To organize a classification or an analysis essay, you need to find a basis for division which does not shift. The divisions should also have the same rank. That sounds tricky, so let me show you what I mean. Here's a sketchy outline that shifts its basis for division:

Types of Aardvarks
Introduction
1 The fuzzy aardvark
2 The hairless aardvark
3 The friendly aardvark
Conclusion

The first two types are divided according to physical characteristics, while the last type is defined by its personality. You see the worry this causes: Can a hairless aardvark be friendly? Are fuzzy aardvarks ill-tempered? How much hair does a friendly aardvark have?

This next skimpy outline demonstrates a shift in rank:

Types of Recorded Music
Introduction
1 Classical
2 Easy listening
3 The Rolling Stones
Conclusion

Although the Rolling Stones represent a type of music distinct from classical and easy listening, the category is not parallel (or equal) to the others; it's too small. It should be rock and roll or hard rock or acid rock, with the Stones used as an example.

Topics for Classification and Analysis Writing

1 Classify the cartoons in the Sunday funnies.
2 What types of TV shows are the most popular this season? Analyze the appeal of each type.

3 Contemplate a magazine advertisement or a television commercial. What emotions and thoughts is this advertising designed to appeal to?

4 Choose a hero you've had in your lifetime and analyze what qualities made this person your idol.

5 If you've ever been a salesperson, waitress, or waiter, how would you classify your customers?

6 Divide into types and analyze any one of these subjects: neighborhoods, marriages, laughter, dreams, teachers, students, tennis players, drinkers, pet owners.

7 Explain what qualities would make up the ideal roommate, dinner date, novel, Saturday afternoon, parent, child, spouse.

Definition

You will always need to define any abstract or controversial terms that figure importantly in your writing. Sometimes this requires only a sentence or two. But sometimes definition can become the structural basis for an entire paper, as when you're isolating, analyzing, and defining a social group such as bores, hippies, or hockey fans. Florence King in the April 1974 issue of *Harper's* presents an extended definition of "The Good Ole Boy," which she organizes using description, narration, and analysis:

THESIS: **The Good Ole Boy is a Southern WASP type, easy to recognize but difficult to define.**

1 Description of general physical characteristics
   A   Middle-aged, jowlish
   B   Drinks beer, wears white socks, etc.
2 Good Ole Boys I have known
   A   Pearl—the playful masher
   B   Calhoun—the kindly fascist
3 Analysis of Good Ole Boy behavior
   A   The Little Dinky syndrome
   B   The search for an oversexed Melanie
   C   An excursion to Johnny's Cash 'n' Carry tavern

Another method of developing a definition involves exclusion, i.e., explaining what something is *not*. If you're going to argue, for instance, that society needs protection from lethal bores, you might begin by presenting examples of several kinds of bores who are bearable, making clear that these are *not* the ones from whom we need protection. Then you zero in on what constitutes a really paralyzing bore, identifying several types and offering more examples. Finally, if possible, mention suggestions for coping with the problem, ideally something more humane than the electric chair.

Topics for Writing Definitions

1 Think of a word or phrase that you use a lot, and then define what you mean by it in different situations.
2 Define a slang term and discuss its possible origins and significance.
3 Define a certain type of person. Examples: the perfectionist, the male chauvinist, the intellectual, the slob, the egomaniac, the life-of-the-party.
4 Write about a term you feel is used in more than one way. Examples: love, friend, materialism, hippie, ugly.
5 Write the definition of an abstract concept. Examples: alienation, eccentricity, power, happiness, progressive, loving.

Comparison and Contrast

One of the most common methods of organization involves focusing on similarities and differences—or more likely on one or the other—in order to make a point. Sometimes we use this technique to clarify: an effective way, for instance, to explain impressionism in literature is to compare it with impressionism in painting, which is visual and hence easier to grasp. Sometimes we use a comparison to persuade, as Naomie Weisstein does in her article, "Woman as Nigger," in the October 1969 issue of *Psychology Today*. Weisstein sets up this analogy in an attempt to jolt readers into seeing that women are conditioned with the slave mentality and exploited for the economic benefit of society just like black people.

When we focus on differences, we often seek to show that one category is somehow better than the other. You could establish a useful comparison between two products, focusing on their differences, in order to recommend one as a better buy than the other. Or you could

humorously contrast the differences between toads and snakes in order
to contend that toads make more companionable pets than snakes.

Whether focusing on differences or similarities, you have two
ways of organizing a comparison or contrast paper. If, for instance,
you decide to contrast the relative merits of toads and snakes, you can
simply list and illustrate all the ingratiating characteristics of toads first.
Then, using a single transition (something like "Snakes, on the other
hand, seldom inspire affection"), you repeat the criteria for snakes,
emphasizing their lack of congeniality. Your conclusion needs only to
prod your reader to observe that, indeed, as you have shown, toads do
make more lovable pets than snakes and don't bite in the bargain.

That's the easy way. A more elaborate way involves establishing
the comparison point by point, as shown in this outline:

THESIS: **Toads make more desirable pets than snakes.**

I Personality traits
   A Snakes
       1 Messy, lose their skins
       2 Introverted, noncommunicative
       3 Speak only in a menacing hiss
   B Toads
       1 Clean, tidy
       2 Placid, undeceptive
       3 Speak in a warm, friendly croak
II Physical characteristics
   A Snakes
       1 Fixed, glassy stare
       2 No ears or legs, loathsome forked tongue
       3 Difficult to cuddle
   B Toads
       1 Large, languid eyes
       2 Quaintly bowlegged
       3 Plump, soft, snuggly

If you're an inexperienced writer, you might do well to try the easy
method first and work up to the sustained, point-by-point contrast.

You'll find another point-by-point comparison outline (this one
on a serious topic) on pages 34–35.

Topics for Comparison and Contrast Writing

1 Discuss one or more illusions that are presented as reality on television and compare the illusion with the reality as you know it.
2 Compare and contrast: two lifestyles you have experienced, two artists, two films, a film and the book it was based on, two people (e.g., two of your friends, two television characters, a friend and an enemy).
3 Compare how you perceived some person, place, or situation as a child with how you perceive the same thing today.
4 Write about a situation in which you expected one thing and got another—in other words, the expectation and the reality were different. Many times these situations are "firsts": your first day of school, your first roommate, your first wedding, your first health food restaurant.
5 Find a typical magazine for men and one for women. Discuss three or four major differences that distinguish these publications.

Cause and Effect

When you develop a topic by analyzing *causes*, you are explaining to your readers why something happened. If you go on to explore the consequences of that happening, you are organizing your analysis of the *effects*. Probably you'll want to content yourself with doing only one or the other in a single piece of writing, but you might attempt both if you should get turned loose without a word limit.

You may be able to fall back on chronological arrangement if you can trace the causes from earliest to most recent. If you're explaining "Why my honeymoon was a disaster," you might trace the cause back to the moment you decided to get married and then pinpoint several unfortunate decisions that followed, like this:

1 My first small mistake: I got engaged (cite details).
2 My next big blunder: I decided to have an elaborate wedding (cite details).
3 My final egregious error: I got smashed at the reception (cite details).

More likely, though, your organization will fall into some simple, logical pattern that has more to do with the importance of the causes or effects than simply with chronology—as from the least significant to the most important. Or from the fairly obvious to the exceedingly subtle. Or from local causes to nationwide causes. The possibilities are endless. Simply present your ideas in the order you consider most clear and emphatic.

If you're seriously analyzing causes or effects, you must be wary of logical fallacies—especially oversimplification and the old post hoc pitfall. Do not write a syllable until you've consulted Chapter 6, especially pages 97 to 101.

Topics for Cause and Effect Writing

1 A group of extraterrestrial beings visits Earth. On their planet people are neither male nor female: each person is both. Using one of these beings as a first-person narrator, explain how their society is different from ours.
2 Explain what causes some natural phenomenon (for example: rain, dew, blue sky, twinkling stars, sweat, hiccups, the phases of the moon).
3 Describe a failure you once had, and tell its causes or effects (or both).
4 Explain the causes (or effects) of any drastic change of opinion, attitude, or behavior you've undergone in your life.
5 Investigate and discuss the possible causes for any opinion, prejudice, interest, or unreasonble fear that you feel strongly.

Persuasion and Argumentation

Persuasion refers to provocative appeals to emotion; *argumentation* refers to logical appeals to reason. In everyday language, the terms are used almost interchangeably; they are used that way here, also, to simplify matters. Most of what we write is intended to be persuasive to some degree. At least it should have a point. Sometimes, though, we write for purely persuasive reasons: We hope to get our readers to agree with our point of view on a debatable subject. That's the kind of writing this section deals with.

Any or all of the organizational patterns covered so far can be used to persuade your readers or to argue a point. Usually you will combine many patterns of development when you write a persuasive paper. You will also need to give extra consideration to your purpose and your audience. Be charming. Be persuasive.

If you're writing on any sort of controversial topic, you'll do well to familiarize yourself with both sides. Not only will you understand the issue better this way, but you'll be able to deal more effectively with the opposing viewpoints—some of which may be lodged firmly in your readers' minds. Your best bet for convincing the nonbelievers is to adopt a rational tone and trot out plenty of telling evidence for your side. But you may first want to present briefly the case for the opposition in order to demolish it with your own irrefutable evidence, clinching your argument with a compelling restatement of your thesis. Or, if you're up to it, use the contrast pattern (page 30) for your outline; present point by point the opposing argument followed point by point with your own, making clear the failings of the opposition while emphasizing the validity of your own.

Topics for Persuasive Writing

1 Partners in a marriage should (should not) write their own detailed marriage contracts.
2 Marriage is (is not) an outmoded custom.
3 Think of one of our popular maxims—like "Absence makes the heart grow fonder" or "Love is never having to say you're sorry." Write about whether you consider the message truth or propaganda, and why.
4 Argue for the alteration or abolition of one of our culture's rituals. Examples: traditional wedding ceremonies, funerals, high school graduation ceremonies, Christmas gift giving, proms, baby showers, presidential elections, dating, beauty contests, and so on.
5 Argue for public ownership of now privately owned services, such as electric companies, phone companies, oil companies, railroads, airlines, and hospitals. Or argue for private ownership of now publicly owned services, like the U.S. Postal Service.

ORGANIZING ESSAY EXAMINATIONS

While you are in college, you may be called upon to use your composition skills as often in writing essay examinations as in composing actual papers. The technique is exactly the same: You still need a thesis statement, and you still need to plan your main points quickly—either in your head or on scratch paper. Finding a thesis presents no problem since you are usually supplied with one. Simply turn the question or topic into a statement, and there you have it. You may want to sharpen the focus if time permits, but always begin by restating the question as a thesis.

You might employ any of the patterns of organization just discussed in ordering your response. Suppose you are asked, ''What were the major political events leading up to the Spanish Civil War?'' You'll probably write a chronologically arranged answer quite automatically. Often essay exam questions request comparisons or contrasts. Suppose you have to deal with a topic like this one: ''Discuss the major differences between Puritanism and Transcendentalism in America.'' If you're writing in class and are pressed for time, you'll do well to organize your answer the easy way: Set down all the important elements of Puritanism; then, using a single transition, present *in the same order* the main elements of Transcendentalism.

But if you should be given a take-home exam, you can at your leisure think of three or four major points on which to set up the contrast; then trot out examples for each movement alternately under these generalizations, something like this:

THESIS: **The major differences between American Puritanism and Transcendentalism involve several basically opposing attitudes.**

I   Attitude toward human nature.
  A   Puritanism considers human nature corrupt.
    1   ''In Adam's Fall we sinned all.''
    2   Doctrine of Original Sin.
  B   Transcendentalism views human nature as essentially good.
    1   Rejects idea of the fall of humanity.
    2   Declares human nature perfectible.
II   Attitude toward God and salvation.
  A   Puritanism sees God above as sovereign ruler.
    1   Chief end of humanity is to glorify God.
    2   Bible is sole authority on religion and morality.
    3   No one is saved by good works—only by divine election.

     B Transcendentalism finds God everywhere.
        1 God is in Nature and within each person.
        2 One comes to know God through "intuition" and the study of Nature.
III Attitude toward society.
     A Puritanism enforces conformity.
        1 Little tolerance for beliefs and customs of others.
        2 Each person responsible for overseeing behavior of neighbors.
     B Transcendentalism encourages self-reliance.
        1 Rejects traditional authority.
        2 Advises individuals to follow decrees of their own consciences.

This outline should certainly produce a complete and well-organized response to an essay examination topic. It should, in fact, produce a good paper in its own right. There really is no difference in the writing process.

Naturally you can't hope to dash off an outline as complete as the one above when you must write in class, but remember that spending a short time thinking through what you're going to say—that is, planning your main points—can greatly improve your response, and thus your grade, on essay exams.

Chapter 3

Compose Pleasing Paragraphs

Your paper will be made up of paragraphs: first, a brief, fascinating introduction; then several interesting, unified, well-developed body paragraphs; and finally, a splendid, emphatic conclusion. Since the opening and closing paragraphs require special attention, let's begin with them.

ADVICE ABOUT INTRODUCTIONS

A friend once told Robert Benchley, the humorist, that introductions were easy if you knew how to start. All you had to do was type "the" at the top of the page, and the rest would come by itself. Next morning Benchley tried it. Tap, tap, tap, t-h-e. Nothing came. He thought, he fidgeted, he fretted, he chewed his nails and popped his knuckles. Finally, in exasperation, he typed "hell with it" and abandoned the project.

Unlike Benchley, you cannot afford the luxury of abandonment. But postponing the introduction until you've gathered momentum and are writing at the height of your powers is probably a good idea. You already know the main idea of your paper (otherwise you couldn't begin writing it), so scrawl your thesis statement across the top of that blank page and get going on the first section of your outline. Think about the introduction in spare moments. Solicit divine inspiration, if possible. Should your introduction still be unfinished when the paper itself is done, you will find that a deadline looming ahead serves wonderfully to focus the mind.

State Your Main Idea

While engaging your readers' attention is an important element of introductory paragraphs, their primary function is to let your readers know what that piece of writing is about. You won't always need a bold statement of your thesis, but the more formal the writing, the more likely you'll need a straightforward statement. In the following introduction, the writer comes directly to the point:

> Today in the United States there is one profession in which conflict of interest is not merely ignored but loudly defended as a necessary concomitant of the free enterprise system. That is in medicine, particularly in surgery.
>
> —(George Crile, Jr., ''The Surgeon's Dilemma,'' *Harper's* (May 1975)

This whole introductory paragraph consists of only his thesis statement since the second sentence just concludes the idea begun in the first. It's really point-blank as introductions go.

Normally, you'll take several sentences to introduce your controlling idea. You can give a little background information or begin with some fairly broad remarks about your subject, then narrow the focus down to the specific idea covered by your thesis. You can see this method illustrated in the following example. (Thesis statements are italicized throughout this section.)

> To her, tight jeans and no bra mean she's in style. To him, they mean she wants to have sex. So it goes among adolescents in Los Angeles, according to a survey by four researchers at U.C.L.A. Despite unisex haircuts, the women's movement, and other signs of equality between the sexes, *boys still read more sexual come-ons into girls' behavior than the girls intend.*
>
> —*Psychology Today* (October 1980)

The article then presents other examples of dress and behavior that are often misinterpreted, just as the introduction promises. Be sure to give your readers at least the main idea of what your essay is going to be about somewhere near the beginning.

Get Your Readers' Attention

If you're going to write skillfully, you need an introduction that makes your prospective readers eager to peruse your essay. You need to capture their interest at the outset.

Use Fascinating Facts   You can catch your readers' attention with facts and statistics—if you can find some real eye-openers like the ones in this introduction to an essay on the need for gun-control laws:

> Every two-and-a-half minutes someone in the United States is robbed at gunpoint, and every forty minutes someone else is murdered with a gun. The weapons find their way into the hands of the criminals in a manner that almost nobody understands. Made in factories owned and operated by the most secretive industry in the country, the guns move through various markets and delivery systems, all of them obscure. Each year police seize about 250,000 handguns and long guns (rifles and shotguns) from the people they arrest. *Given the number of guns that the manufacturers produce each year (2.5 million long guns and 4 million handguns) the supply-and-demand equation works against the hope of an orderly society.*
>
> —Steven Brill, ''The Traffic (Legal
> and Illegal) in Guns,''
> *Harper's* (September 1977)

Pose an Interesting Question   Another way to arrest your readers' attention is by asking a tantalizing question—or maybe a whole series of them, as does the writer of this introduction for a *Newsweek* article:

> Do Whitey Ford and Mickey Mantle *really* favor Miller's new Lite beer over all the others and hoist it off-camera as well as on? And how about Morris, the finicky cat? Does he dart for that other bowl of cat food once the floodlights fade? *Starting in mid-July, Whitey, Mickey, Morris and other celebrity hucksters better be prepared to back up their television-commercial claims by*

actually drinking, eating, or using the products they advertise—or answer to the Federal Trade Commission.

—"Say It's Really So, Joe!" *Newsweek*, June 2, 1975

Notice how handy those rhetorical questions are for sneaking in the main idea. You pose a question, then answer it yourself, and you're off. But be reasonable. Don't use something simpleminded (like "What is sorority life?" or "Were you ever so mad you could scream?") just because it's an easy way to get started.

Imply Your Thesis Occasionally

In narrative and descriptive essays your thesis idea is often so easy to grasp that you don't want to state it directly. Here's an example of an implied thesis from *Harper's* "Wraparound" section (April 1975). The author, who is not a professional writer, by the way, is simply leading up to the details of his disillusionment with his new car:

Watching the auto ads on TV is pretty much like visiting a zoo or a game preserve. After observing leopards and other ferocious felines perform seductive antics for some time, I succumbed and went to a Chevrolet salesroom to get one of these creatures. Unfortunately, the station wagon I purchased did not belong to the cat family. It was a dog.

The double meaning in the slang use of *dog* is a touch that any reader will likely appreciate, probably sympathize with.

And my sympathy to you, as you're sweating out your introduction. Herbert Gold once complained about a similar difficulty—trying to make literature interesting to students. "Moses," he sighed, "only had to bring the Law down the mountain to the children of Israel; I had to bring it pleasingly." If you should manage to come up with something pleasing, you'll be rewarded with a feeling of satisfaction. You can count on that. Probably the only joy involved in writing comes from doing it well.

ADVICE ABOUT CONCLUSIONS

Like introductions, conclusions ought to be forceful and to the point. Work especially hard on your last paragraph. Its effectiveness will influence the way your readers react to the whole paper. If you trail off tiredly at the end, they will sigh and feel let down. Avoid any sort of apology or hedging at this point. Don't end with a whimper. You want something impressive, but don't overdo it.

Conclude Concisely

In fact, if you're writing a short paper and have saved your strongest point for the end, you may not need a whole new paragraph in conclusion. Instead, a sentence or two at the end of the final paragraph providing a sense of closure will do nicely. Here, for example, is the conclusion of Joan Didion's essay analyzing her experiences with migraine headaches. The first part of the paragraph continues describing her suffering, but then shifts (''For when the pain recedes . . .'') to convey her final point—her acceptance of ''the usefulness of migraine.''

> And once it comes, now that I am wise in its ways, I no longer fight it. I lie down and let it happen. At first every small apprehension is magnified, every anxiety a pounding terror. Then the pain comes, and I concentrate only on that. Right there is the usefulness of migraine, there in that imposed yoga, the concentration on the pain. For when the pain recedes, ten or twelve hours later, everything goes with it, all the hidden resentments, all the vain anxieties. The migraine has acted as a circuit breaker, and the fuses have emerged intact. There is a pleasant convalescent euphoria. I open the windows and feel the air, eat gratefully, sleep well. I notice the particular nature of a flower in a glass on the stair landing. I count my blessings.

> —''In Bed,'' from *The White Album* (1979)

Restate Your Thesis Only When Necessary

If you've written something long and informative, like a term paper of ten to twenty typed pages, you'll do well to summarize and restate your main idea. What you want, of course, is a tidy ending that reinforces the point you set out to make in the beginning. The writer of *Psychology Today's* article on misinterpreting sexual signals (the introduction is on page 37) closes with a reinforcement of the thesis:

> The young people's ethnic backgrounds, ages, and previous dating and sexual experiences had almost no effect on their reactions. The girls' ''relatively

less-sexualized view of social relationships,'' the psychologists suggest, ''may reflect some discomfort . . . with the demands of the dating scene''; women do, after all, have more to lose from sexual activity, facing risks of pregnancy and/or a bad reputation. The girls in the study were much more likely than the boys to agree with the statement, ''Sometimes I wish that guys and girls could just be friends without worrying about sexual relationships.''

The quotation at the end reflects the thesis idea (''. . . boys still read more sexual come-ons into girls' behavior than the girls intend''), but does so in quite different terms and in a touching way.

Try an Echo

If you can bring it off, the technique of echoing some element from your introduction is an especially good one. It gives your essay unity. The *Newsweek* article about a new policy requiring people or pets who push products to actually use them concludes with a reference to the same celebrities mentioned in the introduction (on page 38):

> Most advertisers do not feel that the proposed regulations will cramp their style. In any event, it is unlikely to have much effect on Mantle and Ford, who are known to like their beer, and Morris seems honestly to savor 9-Lives cat food. But the rule could have posed a problem for Joe Namath, the nonpareil quarterback. Until recently, he did commercials for Beauty Mist pantyhose.

Offer Encouragement

Often you can fittingly close with a few words of encouragement for your readers. Tell them how delicious they will find the cheesecake if they follow your instructions to the letter. Or how rewarding they will find growing their own tomatoes, as Mark Kane does in this conclusion:

> When you shop for tomato seeds or plants this season, consider trying at least one new variety. There are hundreds to choose from and if you keep looking, one of them may find a home in your garden. Even if you find nothing to match your favorite, you'll have fun, and the pleasure of gardening is not just in the eating.

—''The Tomato: Still Champion,'' *Organic Gardening* (March 1982)

Suggest Solutions

If you're writing analysis or argument, a useful closing device involves offering suggestions—possible solutions for problems discussed in the essay. This technique is valid only if you can come up with sound ideas for solving problems. Steven Brill ends his article about the proliferation of guns in the United States (the introduction is on page 38) with some practical suggestions:

> All these small steps toward sanity are possible if we force the people who profit from America's free-wheeling gun traffic to be open, accountable, and fully responsible to law-enforcement needs. If we're going to continue to allow the RGs or the Smith and Wessons to make guns at all for civilian use, we ought to at least demand that they become partners in the effort to curb the carnage their weapons cause. When we think of people murdered or robbed at gunpoint, we have to start thinking of brand names.

Just be sure, though, that your suggestions are truly sound ideas, not facile advice borrowed from a TV commercial or a Hallmark card.

Provide a Warning

At some time you may desire to inform your fellow citizens about a grave danger which they are comfortably ignoring—AIDS, acid rain, nuclear waste, chemical dumps, or the arms race. Then your conclusion can appropriately be a warning, something similar to the following paragraph, the final one in an article written by Dr. Richard Champlin, a specialist in bone marrow transplants. Although Dr. Champlin's article describes the plight of dying radiation victims following the Chernobyl nuclear power plant disaster in 1986, notice that he takes the opportunity in his conclusion to broaden the context of his warning:

> The disaster at Chernobyl demonstrated the devastating effects of radiation exposure. It illustrates the fact that adequate medical care would be impossible in a larger nuclear catastrophe. As a cancer doctor, I'm accustomed to dealing with patients who die. This was different; I was *overwhelmed* by the human suffering. But the fact is that the damage and human misery that would be wrought by nuclear weapons would be immeasurably worse. Chernobyl would pale by comparison.

—"With the Chernobyl Victims,"
Los Angeles Times Magazine (July 6, 1986)

Conclusions aren't really all that difficult. Often they turn out weak because we write them last, when our powers are under a cloud. Treat your conclusion like your introduction: think about it off and on while you're writing the paper—during coffee breaks or whenever you pause to let your mind rest. Jot down anything promising that comes to you. Concentrate on the conclusion, just as you will on the introduction, when you revise.

ADVICE ABOUT BODY PARAGRAPHS

If you are doing academic, business, or technical writing, the paragraphs that constitute the body of your paper should each have a topic sentence supported by plenty of concrete details. A friend of mine says that all through college she got her papers back with "Underde-veloped ¶" scrawled in the margins. To correct this problem, she would carefully restate the topic four or five different ways in each paragraph, and she'd still get "Underdeveloped ¶" marked in her margins.

My friend finally realized, too late, what *underdevelopment* meant. She wonders why her teachers never wrote in her margins, "Add an example or illustration here," or "Give some specific details," or "Describe your reasoning step by step." She would have understood *that*.

When you find one of your skimpy paragraphs marked *under-nourished* or ¶ *devel*, you'll know what it means: Add examples, provide specific details, describe your reasoning, or do all three.

Use Topic Sentences in Informative Writing

Put the topic sentence first whenever you write to inform—that is, in doing summaries, reports, academic papers, and examinations. When you're composing narratives or descriptions, you may often imply your topic sentence, just as you imply your thesis statement in those modes of writing. Like the thesis sentence for an essay, a topic sentence states the controlling idea for the paragraph. The details within that paragraph will support, illustrate, expand, explain, or justify that idea. If you follow your unified outline, you will automatically write unified paragraphs. But if you need to dredge up more details while in the process of writing the paper, be sure those additions are to the point—i.e., that they pertain to the idea stated in the topic sentence.

If, for instance, you are planning a paragraph about the undeserved reputation of dogs, you might use this topic sentence: "Far from being one's best friends, dogs tend to be slow-witted, servile, slobbering beasts seldom deserving of their board and keep." Next you need to trot out examples of slavish spaniels and doltish Great Danes you have known in order to convince your readers that dogs make wretched companions. But if you then observe, "Cats are pretty contemptible also," you need a new paragraph. Or else you need to toss that bit of evidence out as being beside the point, the *point* being whatever idea you committed yourself to in the topic sentence. You can, of course, broaden the topic sentence if you decide cats are essential to your argument. You can expand the topic sentence to read something like this: "Both dogs and cats are exceedingly disagreeable creatures to have around the house." Now the way is clear to discuss all the skittish cats of your acquaintance as well as those loutish dogs in a comparison and contrast paragraph.

Furnish the Facts and Figures

Supply enough examples to convince your readers that what you assert is true. If you say that members of Congress have too many special privileges, then *prove* it. Mention that Congress members enjoy free medical care at taxpayers' expense. Mention that Senate restaurants in 1975 were subsidized by the taxpayers to the tune of $240,000. Mention that plants and flowers to beautify congressional offices set the taxpayers back $1.2 million each year.[1] Convince your readers that these expenditures and many more are unnecessary to the orderly function of government. Insist that members of Congress should pay their own way, just like the rest of us. Don't expect your readers to take your word about anything without evidence, though. They won't— unless they just happened to agree with you in the first place.

Notice how the plentiful details in the following paragraph allow us to see clearly how the McDonald's chain pioneered in delivering fast food:

The new McDonald's system was predicated on careful attention to detail. The McDonald brothers shortened the spindles on their Multi-Mixers so that

---

[1]These facts and figures, by the way, come from Robert Shrum's "The Imperial Congress," *New Times*, March 18, 1977, pp. 20–34.

shakes and malts could be made directly in paper cups; there would be no metal mixing containers to wash, no wasted ingredients, no wasted motion, no wasted time. They developed dispensers that put the same amount of catsup or mustard on every bun. They installed a bank of infrared lamps to keep French fries hot. They used disposable paper goods instead of glassware and china. They installed a microphone to amplify the customer's voice and reduce misunderstandings about what was being ordered. By 1952 the McDonald brothers' employees, all men dressed neatly in white, were said to be capable of serving the customer a hamburger, a beverage, French fries, and ice cream in twenty seconds. Word of their proficiency began to spread through the restaurant industry.

> —Philip Langdon, "Burgers! Shakes!"
> *Atlantic Monthly* (December 1985)

Include Concrete Details

Whenever possible, use examples that your readers can *visualize*. If you say that motorcycle riding can be dangerous, mention the crushed noses, the dislocated limbs, the splintered teeth, the crushed skulls. Be as concrete and specific as possible. You can't avoid abstractions entirely, of course, but try to follow abstract words—like *dangerous*—with concrete illustrations—like *broken bones*.

You must be especially wary of abstract terms like *democracy*, *truth*, *justice*, *liberty*, and such familiar-sounding words. They mean different things to different people. And sometimes they convey little meaning at all. Consider the following paragraph which purports to explain what a "democratic" education can do for a child:

> A democratic plan of education includes more than the mere transmission of the social heritage and an attempt to reproduce existing institutions in a static form. The purpose of democratic education is the development of well-integrated individuals who can live successfully in an ever-changing dynamic culture. The democratic school is also required to indoctrinate individuals with the democratic tradition which, in turn, is based on the agitative liberties of the individual and the needs of society.

No reader can be expected to make sense out of that string of abstract ideas. If you can divine meaning there, it is a vague, shadowy sort of understanding that can't be pinned down precisely because of the numerous abstract words: *democratic*, *social heritage*, *well-integrated*, *dynamic culture*. And what *agitative liberties* are, only the writer knows. He didn't provide us with even a hint. The entire passage contains not a single concrete example to help us grasp the ideas that he was trying to express. You need to train yourself to write in concrete terms as much as possible and to provide definitions and examples when you have to deal with abstractions.

Particularly in writing research papers, you must guard against the tendency to omit examples. Since you are reading widely and condensing material, you'll naturally be leaving out a lot for the sake of compression. What you'll probably be leaving out most often will be the examples. Remember that in order for your own writing to be as convincing as that in your sources, you must get some of those examples back in—either those from the original or some new ones of your own.

KEEP YOUR READERS WITH YOU: COHERENCE

As you are writing along on your paper following your outline (having either mastered the introduction or postponed it for later), you may encounter another minor difficulty in tying your major points together. Again, remember to keep your readers in mind. You want them to understand what you're writing and understand it easily on the first reading. So, don't let your readers get lost when you move from one idea to the next or when you change the direction of your ideas. The things you do to make your paper hang together, to make it *coherent*, are relatively simple; yet they can often mean the difference between a first-rate paper and a merely passable one.

DON'T LOSE US ON THE TURNS: TRANSITIONS

The abiding principle of good coherence lies in presenting your ideas in an orderly fashion and then providing transitions when you go from one idea to the next. All this means is that you put up verbal signs showing your readers that you're moving to another point, which usually means to the next section of your outline. The indention for a new paragraph does this to a certain extent. But indenting could also mean that you're going to amplify the same idea. And often your thought changes direction in the middle of a paragraph when you're organizing through contrast or when you add examples or note an exception.

These signals can be as pointed as "Next let us consider the problem of . . ." or "As I have shown in this paper. . . ." That's pretty obvious and creaky transition. You can do better. Figure 3-1 provides a slew of transitional words neatly classified according to meaning. Take note of the different types of transitions illustrated; then tuck in a bookmark in case you get stuck and need a transition to help you over a rough spot.

Be careful, though, not to overuse these transitional terms or your prose will be plodding. Here are some other ploys for slipping smoothly from one paragraph to the next.

Try a Rhetorical Question

If you're stuck for a logical way to lead from one point to the next, you can occasionally pose a question and then answer it, like this:

> How do we stop people from breeding? First, by not constantly brainwashing the average girl into thinking that motherhood must be her supreme experience. Very few women are capable of being good mothers; and very few men of being good fathers. Parenthood is a gift, as most parents find out too late and most children find out right away. So a change in attitude will help; and that seems to be happening.
>
> Gore Vidal, "The State of the Union,"
> *Esquire* (May 1975)

Or as a last resort, you can fall back on "The question now arises . . . ," which allows you to inject your new idea. Say you're discussing dope addiction among the young. You've just proved satisfactorily that this is a problem. You slide into your next point by writing, "The question now is, what can society do to discourage drug use among teenagers?" Then you trot out one by one the preventive measures that you think might be effective. This device, useful though it is, will seldom work more than one time per paper. You must have others in stock.

The Short-Sentence Transition

Like the rhetorical question, the short-sentence transition must not be used often but comes in handy when you need it. You simply state

Figure 3-1   Useful transitional terms.

To move to the next major point: *too, moreover, in the first place, next, second, third, again, besides, in addition, further, likewise, finally, beyond this, admittedly, like*

Examples: We can see *also* that the quality of most television programs is abysmal.
Furthermore, the commercials constantly assault our taste and insult our intelligence.

To add an example: *for example, such as, that is, in the following manner, namely, in this case, as an illustration, at the same time, in addition*

Examples: The daytime game shows, *for instance*, openly appeal to human greed.
Soap operas, *in the same manner*, pander to many of our baser instincts.

To emphasize a point: *especially, without doubt, primarily, chiefly, actually, otherwise, after all, as a matter of fact, more importantly*

Examples: The constant violence depicted on television, *in fact*, poses a danger to society.
Even more offensive are deodorant commercials, *without question* the most tasteless on TV.

To contrast a point: *but, still, on the other hand, on the contrary, nevertheless, contrary to, however, nonetheless, conversely, in contrast, neither*

Examples: We abhor the violence, yet we don't like censorship.
Although commercials may enrage or sicken us, they do, *after all*, pay the bills.
Granted that advertising picks up the tab, the deceptiveness of commercials remains indefensible.

To conclude a point: *consequently, so, accordingly, then, hence, as a result, in sum, in conclusion, in other words, finally, at last, after all*

Examples: Soap operas *thus* contribute to the subtle erosion of moral values.
Commercials, *therefore*, are not worth the sacrifice of our integrity.
Television, *in short*, costs more than society should be willing to pay.

briefly and graciously in advance what you intend to discuss next, like this:

> Europeans think more highly of Americans now than they ever did. Let me try to explain why.

> —Anthony Burgess, ''Is America Falling Apart?''
> *New York Times Magazine* (November 7, 1971)

John Kenneth Galbraith uses a slightly more formal version:

> Economics, foreign policy, the split in the party as it relates to racial equality, and some resulting questions of political style all require a special word. To these matters I now turn.

> —''Who Needs the Democrats?'' *Harper's* (July 1970)

Something Subtle for the Skillful: Echo Transitions

Often you won't need such obvious transitions. The smoothest and the most effective method involves touching on the idea from your previous paragraph as you pick up and introduce the idea for your next one. Sounds tricky, I know, but it's worth working on if you want to write readable prose. Pay close attention to these examples. The first one gives you the final sentence from a paragraph by Frederick Lewis Allen about the big Red scare in the twenties, and it is followed by the opening sentence of his next paragraph which explains the reasons for the scare. The transitional words are italicized. Notice how ''this national panic'' refers back to ''a reign of terror,'' while at the same time leading into the new idea of justification for the scare:

> It was an era of lawless and disorderly defense of law and order, of unconstitutional defense of the Constitution, of suspicion and civil conflict— in a very literal sense, *a reign of terror.*

> For *this national panic* there was a degree of justification.

> —*Only Yesterday* (1931, p. 39)

The next example is taken from Stewart Alsop's analysis of the drug problem in New York City. You have the last two sentences of his paragraph citing the monetary cost of heroin addiction, followed by the opening sentence of the next paragraph. Note that Alsop repeats the same key phrase:

> . . . addicts must steal more than $1.5 billion from the people of New York every year. But that sum is a tiny fraction of *the real cost*.
>
> *The real cost* is the death of New York as a city in which people who have any choice at all will be willing to live.

> —"The Smell of Death," *Newsweek* (February 1, 1971, p. 76)

Here is an example from James Baldwin. Notice that the transitional phrase "this perpetual dealing with people" in the opening sentence of the new paragraph refers back to the whole idea stated in the last sentence of the previous paragraph. At the same time, the phrase leads smoothly into his next point—how this wide acquaintance with people helped to get rid of his preconceived ideas:

> I love to talk to people, all kinds of people, and almost everyone, as I hope we still know, loves a man who loves to listen.
> *This perpetual dealing with people* very different from myself caused a shattering in me of preconceptions I scarcely knew I held.

> —*Nobody Knows My Name* (Dial Press, 1959)

In the final example, Katherine Anne Porter combines an echo with a regular transitional sentence to gain emphasis. She's writing about the peaceful protests preceding the execution of Sacco and Vanzetti in 1927. The paragraph just concluding here describes the frightening tactics of the mounted police:

> I do not believe the police meant for the hoofs to strike and crush heads—it was just a very showy technique for intimidating and controlling a *mob*.
>
> This was not a *mob*, however. It was a silent, intent assembly of citizens. . . .

> —Katherine Anne Porter, "The Never-Ending Wrong,"
> *Atlantic Monthly* (June 1977)

Echoes within Paragraphs

You don't have to work as hard on transitions *within* paragraphs, since most of these echoes occur automatically. But it's well to understand the process in case you have to patch up a paragraph sometime. Mainly transition within paragraphs occur through words deliberately repeated and the echo of pronouns as they refer back to their antecedents. You may, also, use any of the standard techniques for achieving transition between paragraphs. In the following example, I've italicized the typical transitional devices and have used capital letters to show the repetition of the key term ADDICT and the unfortunately sexist pronouns that refer to it:

> *What to do about drug addiction?* I give you two statistics. England with a population of over fifty-five million has eighteen hundred ADDICTS. The United States with over two hundred million has nearly five hundred thousand ADDICTS. *What are the English doing right that we are doing wrong?* They have turned the problem over to the doctors. An ADDICT is required to register with a physician who gives HIM at controlled intervals a prescription so that HE can buy HIS drug. The ADDICT is content. *Best of all*, society is safe. The Mafia is out of the game. The police are unbribed, and the ADDICT will not mug an old lady in order to get the money for HIS next fix.
>
> —Gore Vidal, "The State of the Union,"
> *Esquire* (May 1975)

Notice that sentences 3 and 4 (both citing statistics) are approximately parallel in structure; i.e., the second echoes the structure of the preceding sentence, which helps give coherence. And besides the repetition of the word ADDICT, we get echoes from *England/English/ they;* from *United States/we/society;* and from *doctors/physicians/who.* Even more subtle are the echoes from *content* and *safe*, words with a similar comforting meaning. It's a nicely coherent paragraph, and you can do as well if you'll put your mind to it.

Remember this, though: Your best chance of getting coherence in your paragraphs over the long haul involves keeping a clear continuity of ideas. You need transitions only to direct the flow.

Chapter 4

Style Your Sentences

The previous chapter explained how to put ideas together into well-developed paragraphs. Those ideas should, of course, be expressed in clear, concise, shapely sentences. Such sentences do not simply flow from a good writer's pen—nor do they appear perfectly formed following the touch of a keyboard. Effective sentences are constructed. They are written and rewritten, moved around, added to, and sometimes scratched out. As you know, this tinkering with words and the ideas they convey is called *revising*, and it is a crucial step in the writing process.

Whether you do this rewriting as you struggle to get through a first draft or whether you postpone it until a second or third draft makes little difference. Do it the way that feels most natural for you—but don't fail to do it.

WRITE NATURALLY, AS YOU SPEAK

Lewis Lapham, editor of *Harper's* magazine, complains: "I have found that few writers learn to speak in the human voice, that most of them make use of alien codes (academic, political, literary, bureaucratic, technical."[1] Strive for a human voice when you write—preferably your own. Many people produce on paper a kind of artificial language that writing specialist Ken Macrorie calls *Engfish*—a language much different from the kind people speak or the kind most professional writers write. Engfish is invariably stuffy and abuses the third-person approach to writing. (Writing in the *third person* means adopting an impersonal approach by using *one*, *he*, *she*, *it*, or *they*, instead of the more personal *I*, *we*, or *you*.) Engfish sounds like this:

> One can observe that athletics can be beneficial to the health of one who participates as well as entertaining for one who watches.

Put that sentence into English and you get:

> Athletics can be healthful for the players and entertaining for the fans.

Eventually you must master the third-person approach without lapsing into Engfish. But unless the occasion requires the formality of third person, I suggest that you use the first-person *I* or *we* (as I just did in this sentence). Most professional writers use *I* and *we* when expressing their own opinions, and many of them address their readers directly as *you*. If you do the same, you'll find Engfish easier to avoid.

Avoid the *Indefinite You*

But take caution: The word *you* should always refer to the readers, unless you intend to be funny. You may get an unexpected laugh if you're explaining how to prune a tree and write, "Grasp your diseased limb firmly and saw it off immediately above the joint." Reserve this *indefinite you* for humorous writing in which no one will mind if you write, "The behavior of your average alligator tends to be torpid."

---

[1]"The Pleasures of Reading," *Harper's*, May 1975, p. 50.

Exercise 4-1

Translate these sentences from Engfish into clear, straightforward English. You may have to guess at the meaning sometimes, but do your best. I'll rewrite the first one to get you started.

1 The causal factors of her poverty become obvious when one considers the number of offspring she possesses.

   Translation: Her poverty is increased because she has so many children.

2 This writer's report enjoyed a not unfavorable reception by the committee.
3 The fire department is requesting additional funds for effective confinement and extinguishment of unwanted and destructive fires.
4 The level of radiation in the immediate vicinity of the nuclear power plant was evaluated and found to be within acceptable danger parameters.
5 Consumer elements are continuing to stress the fundamental necessity of a stabilization of the price structure at a lower level than exists at the present time.
6 The unacceptability of one's lifestyle can result in the termination of one's employment in some firms.
7 Police involvement in the conflict was considered to be an inhibiting factor to the peaceful progress of the protest.
8 It was with no little enthusiasm that one's peers inflicted various contusions and lacerations on members of the opposing affinity group.
9 These new economic statistics have validated the essentiality of the President's policies effected to mitigate the inflation rate.
10 It is the feeling of the committee that the established priorities in management-employee relations are in need of realignment.

USE THE ACTIVE VOICE

If your writing is generally lifeless, turgid, and wordy, the *passive voice* may be the culprit. The passive construction (in which the subject is acted upon instead of doing the acting) is less economical than active voice in conveying the same information:

Passive: Because patriotism was lacking in their hearts, the battle was lost by the mercenaries.
(14 words)

Active: Because they lacked heartfelt patriotism, the mercenaries lost the battle.
(10 words)

That's not many extra words, I'll grant, but if you add only a couple of unnecessary words to each sentence in a paper, you will seriously pollute your prose.

Even when not wordy, the passive construction leaves out information—sometimes essential information. Take this typical concise passive construction:

The prisoner was fed.

That's not an objectionable sentence. Nobody is perishing to know who fed the prisoner. But consider the same sentence with only one word changed:

The prisoner was beaten.

At once we want to know *by whom*? By the sheriff? By one of the deputies? By a guard? By a fellow prisoner? There is no way to tell from the passive construction. In his article "Watergate Lingo," Richard Gambino observes, "The effect of the habitual use of the passive is to create a . . . world where events have lives, wills, motives, and actions of their own without any human being responsible for them."

Notice: It's the *habitual use of the passive* that is treacherous. I do not mean that you should never use the passive voice. Sometimes it can be the best way to convey information. You would likely choose the passive "The President was elected by a comfortable majority" rather than the active "A comfortable majority elected the President." No reader will be troubled by not being told who elected the President because everyone knows that the voters do the electing. The passive is also appropriate when you want to stress that an action is *happening to* or being *inflicted upon* the subject:

The city hall was damaged by an earthquake.

My bicycle was demolished by a truck.

The candidate's credibility has been questioned by the media.

Exercise   **4-2**

Rewrite the following passive sentences in the active voice and eliminate any wordiness. I'll get you started by doing the first one.

1   An empty disposable lighter is used by folksinger Utah Phillips to store
    kitchen matches in.

    Revised: Folksinger Utah Phillips stores kitchen matches in an empty
                    disposable lighter.

2   Several disposable lighters were lost by Seymour last week.
3   It is probable that matches should be used by people who often lose things.
4   Matchbooks have been found to be more versatile than disposable lighters
    by some people.
5   No mail-order opportunities to become electricians, locksmiths, and
    engineers are offered by disposable lighters.
6   How many matches are left in a book can be easily seen by the match
    user.
7   Let our daily bread be given to us this day.
8   It was stated by the author in the introduction that several approaches to
    grammar would be discussed.
9   Several secondary sources were studied in order to gain additional infor-
    mation for this paper.
10 The demand for shirts bearing alligators was artificially stimulated by
    advertising.

Practice the Passive

Despite all my warnings against habitual use of the passive, I'm aware
that writers in a number of jobs and in some academic disciplines are
expected—even required—to use the passive voice. If you are taking
courses in education, corrections, or any of the hard sciences
(chemistry, biology, physics, and the like), you must learn to write

gracefully in the passive voice. It can be done. But you will need to practice diligently.

Proceeding from the pen of an accomplished writer, the passive voice is not in the least objectionable. Jessica Mitford, for one, employs the passive so skillfully that you never notice its presence:

> Today, family members who might wish to be in attendance would certainly be dissuaded by the funeral director.

That sentence will not be noticeably improved by making it active voice:

> Today the funeral director would certainly dissuade family members who might wish to be in attendance.

In order to help you perfect your use of the passive, we have collected some useful and fairly simple sentences as models. If you must become a practitioner of the passive, you'll do well to work this exercise twice, thinking of different material to use the second time.

Writing Exercise   **4-3**

Copy each sentence carefully. Then, choosing subject matter from your academic major, write five sentences imitating the passive structure of each of the originals. Work on them a few at a time. Do two or three, take a break, then come back and do some more. I'll do the first one to give you the idea.

> Certain things were not mentioned.   (Jane O'Reilly)

1 *Imitations:*   Synthetic fertilizers were not unknown.
                   Pesticides were not advised.
                   Crop rotation was not used.
                   Early harvesting was not recommended.
                   Organic methods were not tried.

2 The entire body of a tarantula, especially its legs, is thickly clothed with hair.   (Alexander Petrunkevitch)

3 All others, except apprentices, are excluded by law from the preparation room.   (Jessica Mitford)

4 The poor are slated to take the brunt of the federal budget cuts.   (Barbara Ehrenreich)

5 The SKIP option can be used in input and output statements.   (J. S. Roper)

6 The emphasis is generally put on the right to speak.   (Walter Lippmann)

7 This could be done either by the accumulation of observed evidence or by mathematics.   (Sir Kenneth Clark)

8 But—poor little thing—the boundary ought in its turn to be protected.   (E. M. Forster)

9 Negotiations over a strike of factory workers were conducted among trade union leaders, the minister of labor, and the commander of an infantry brigade.   (Lucy Komisar)

SENTENCE COMBINING

You can enhance a sentence (or a series of sentences) by *subordinating* some of the elements—that is, by tucking less important ideas into dependent clauses and small details into phrases. Thus major ideas are elevated in independent or main clauses, where they receive the proper emphasis.

A Word about Clauses and Phrases

If you're hazy about the meaning of some of those terms I just used, let me explain that an *independent clause* can stand as a sentence all by itself. A *dependent clause*, which begins with a subordinating word (see list, page 203), must be attached to an independent clause (or else it is a *fragment*). In case you're also hazy about the difference between clauses and phrases, remember that a clause has both a subject and a verb; a phrase does not.

Phrases:	having lost my head
	to lose my head
	after losing my head
Clauses:	after I lost my head (*dependent*)
	I lost my head (*independent*)
	that I lost my head (*dependent*)

Subordinating Ideas

Although simple and compound sentences may be the easiest ones to write, they don't always get across the relationships between your ideas in the clearest way possible. And if you use simple sentences too often, you'll have a third-grade writing style. Here are a couple of plain, simple sentences:

> Lucy forgot how to spell *exaggerated*. She used the word *magnified* instead.

The idea in the first of those sentences could be subordinated in these ways:

a By using subordinating conjunctions and adverbs (Examples: *after, when, because, if, while, until, unless*):

> *Since Lucy forgot how to spell exaggerated*, she used the word *magnified* instead.

b By using an adjective clause:

> Lucy, *who forgot how to spell exaggerated*, used the word *magnified* instead.

c By using a participial phrase or an adjective:

> *Having forgotten how to spell exaggerated*, Lucy used the word *magnified* instead.

Combining Sentences to Avoid Repetition

You should consider sentence combining if you find yourself writing too many simple, monotonous sentences or if you see that you are repeating the same word without meaning to, like this:

> The pontoon boat had stalled in the middle of the lake.
>
> The boat stalled because it ran out of gas.

You'll notice when you start to revise that you've got too many *stalled*s and too many *boat*s there. Using subordination, you can combine those sentences and the problem is solved:

> The pontoon boat, which ran out of gas, had stalled in the middle of the lake.

Or, if you want to emphasize the reason the boat was stranded, you can combine the sentences this way:

> The pontoon boat, stalled in the middle of the lake, had run out of gas.

A Word of Warning

Although skillful sentence combining serves to focus your ideas and add sophistication to your style, don't get carried away. *Remember: Clarity is the keynote.* Don't get so enthusiastic in your use of subordination that you try to compress too much into a single sentence and thus obscure your meaning.

Writing Exercise   4-4

The following sentences were written by students. Combine each pair into a single clear, concise sentence.

1 The second type of day is a blah day. Most days, especially in the middle of the semester, fall into this category.
2 While the goals of music therapy are nonmusical, the activities prescribed to reach these goals are musical. Musical activities include singing, listening, playing instruments, writing songs, dancing, and moving.
3 Kate Chopin wrote a short story called "The Storm." As the title suggests, the story is about a savage storm and shows how the characters respond to the downpour.
4 There are three major aspects to consider in examining this character. These aspects include what the author tells us about this character, what she herself says and does, and what other people say to her and about her.
5 Most of the incidents that inspire Walter Mitty's fantasies have humorous associations. These incidents can be broken down into basically two groups, with the first one being his desire to be in charge.

CONSTRUCTING IMPRESSIVE SENTENCES
FOR SPECIAL OCCASIONS

Another good way to make your prose effective involves writing an occasional forceful sentence. If every sentence built to a climax, your readers might well be bowled over, so don't work at it too hard. But in a key position—such as at the beginning or end of a paragraph, or to emphasize a point anytime—a carefully controlled sentence is worth the time it takes to compose it.

Save the Clincher for the End—Periodic Structure

Most of the time we don't deliberate about our sentence structure. We attach ideas together, automatically subordinating the less important ones, until we come to the end of the thought, where we put a period and start in on another one. These everyday sentences—like the one I just wrote—are called "cumulative" and constitute the bulk of our writing. If, however, you need a Sunday-best sentence, you either consciously plan it or later rearrange it: you want to order the details to build to a big finish. You don't disclose your main idea until just before the period, which accounts for the label "periodic." Let me show you the difference with a few examples.

Cumulative:	Seymour made the honor roll while holding down a part-time job and playing the lead in *Hamlet*.
Periodic:	While holding down a part-time job and playing the lead in *Hamlet*, Seymour made the honor roll.
Cumulative:	Our first consideration is the preservation of our environment, even though preventing pollution costs money.
Periodic:	Even though preventing pollution costs money, our first consideration is the preservation of our environment.

If you have a feel for prose, you probably already write periodic sentences when you need them without being aware that you're doing it. If, on the other hand, you're not long on style, you can develop some by cinching up a few of your sentences. Here are a few more pointers.

Try a Short One for Emphasis

The really brief sentence is easier to handle than the periodic sentence and is remarkably effective—as long as you don't overdo it. Often short-short sentences appear at the beginning or at the end of a paragraph, since these are the most emphatic positions. You can lob one in, though, anytime you feel brave enough as long as you have a point to make. Notice the emphasis achieved in the following examples by the short sentence following one of normal length:

Cavett's purpose was to ensure that I would suffer all the shocks, surprises, pitfalls and confusions that afflict the host five shows a week. He succeeded.

—Jesse Birnbaum, *Time* (June 7, 1971)

Webster's dictionaries and the endless multiplication of handbooks and courses in English composition represent a desperate effort to prevent class distinction from revealing itself in language. And, of course, it has failed.

—John H. Fisher, *School and Society* (November 1969)

The short sentence also functions effectively as a transitional device. In the following examples, the short transitional sentences are italicized:

"No man," wrote John Donne, "doth exalt Nature to the height it would beare." He saw the discrepancy between dream and reality.
Great minds have always seen it. That is why man has survived his journey this long.

—Loren Eiseley, *Horizon* (March 1962)

Economics, foreign policy, the split in the party as it relates to racial equality, and some resulting questions of political style all require a special word. *To these matters I now turn.*

—John Kenneth Galbraith, *Harper's* (July 1970)

Experiment with the Dash

Since the end of a sentence is an emphatic position, you can use a dash there to good advantage, as Woodrow Wilson did in this warning: "I have seen their destruction, as will come upon these again—utter destruction and contempt.'' Note the deliberate repetition of the word *destruction*, amplified by *contempt*. The dash can be used to tack on afterthoughts, but you'll find it more effective for reinforcement of a point or for elaboration, like this:

> Hollywood offered the public yet another marvel—talking films.

> This was the year of the big spectaculars—biblical extravaganzas spiced with sex and filmed in glorious Technicolor.

Sometimes you may want to call attention to an idea in midsentence. Again, dashes will do it:

> The President was beginning—though he did not suspect it—his last month in office.

If you prefer *not* to call attention to the thought inserted, use commas instead of dashes:

> The President was altering, though he neglected to tell the press, his firm commitments on foreign aid.

The dash, like the short sentence, can't retain its effect if overused. In fact, a flurry of dashes produces an unfortunate, adolescent style. So experiment with the dash in your first draft. Leave it in only if you're sure it works well.

For more information, look up *Dash* in the ''Revising Index,'' Chapter 8.

Balanced Sentences

Another way to keep your ideas clear and to make them emphatic is to use *balanced sentences* (or *parallel structure*). Balanced sentences depend upon repetition: sometimes of the same words, always of the same grammatical structures—phrases, clauses, now and then whole sentences. Virginia Woolf repeats the same adverb, changing the verb each time to achieve this impressive sentence:

> One cannot think well, love well, sleep well, if one has not dined well.

Mark Twain balances independent clauses for a comic effect in this line spoken by the narrator of "A Dog's Tale":

My father was a St. Bernard, my mother was a collie, but I am a Presbyterian.

For Everyday Writing While parallel structure lends itself particularly well to emphatic sentences, the technique is fundamental to all good writing. If you by chance put together a sentence involving two similar elements or a series of them, your readers *expect* these similar parts to be balanced (or parallel). Such a structure may occur whenever you join parts of sentences with any of the coordinating conjunctions (*and, but, or, for, nor, yet, so*).

Consider the problem first in this simple example:

Clyde likes *to smoke* and *drinking*.

Your readers expect those italicized parts to sound alike, to be balanced in construction, like this:

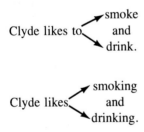

Let's try a more typical example—the kind of sentence you're likely to write in a hurry and should put into parallel structure when you revise:

Politicians today face the difficult tasks of *solving* urban problems and *how to find* the money without raising taxes.

This one is easy to repair. You need to balance the two grammatical structures connected by *and: solving* urban problems and *how to find* the money. The easiest way is to make *how to find* sound the same as *solving*—that is, use *finding*:

Politicians today face the difficult task of *solving* urban problems and *finding* the money without raising taxes.

For Sunday-best Sentences Once you become adept at constructing balanced sentences, you'll find the technique perfect for composing *climactic* sentences—the kind you need to emphasize key points, to conclude paragraphs, and to bring essays to a resounding finish. Martin Luther King, Jr., learned from the Bible how to balance phrases with ringing effect:

With this faith we will be able to work together, to pray together, to struggle together, to go to jail together, to stand up for freedom together, knowing that we will be free one day.

Here's a first-rate concluding sentence written by John Kenneth Galbraith, the noted economist:

To summarize, our present situation is not military need in response to tension and hostility; it is tension and hostility in the service of military need.

—*Harper's* (November 1986)

Parallel structure also provides the most effective way to compress a number of ideas into a single sentence with perfect clarity. In this next example let me show you graphically how *Time*'s drama critic, T. E. Kalem, balances phrases in a sentence about George Bernard Shaw's *Man and Superman*:

Shaw steadily sounds his pet themes:

the chicanery	of politics,
the corruptive power	of money,
the degrading stench	of poverty,
the servile dependencies	of marriage and family,
the charlatanism	of medicine,
the fossilization	of learning,
the tyranny	of the state,
the stupidity	of the military, and

the bigoted, sanctimonious zeal of the church.

There's no other way to deliver so many ideas so clearly in so short a sentence.

You can also use parallel structure to good effect in separate sentences by repeating the same grammatical structure in each sentence. This technique involves building to a climax, which means you can't use it often, but the effect is impressive when well done. Here is Maya Angelou repeating balanced clauses (beginning with *because*) to emphasize the reasons she undervalued the virtues of her race:

> Because Southern black people move slowly, I was quick to think they did not move at all. Because many Southern black people speak in black English, I had taken too lightly the wisdom of their words. Because Southern black Americans had employed a gargantuan patience, I had not fully appreciated the splendor of their survival.

Finally, notice how Pastor Martin Niemoeller, a Lutheran minister, achieves eloquence by using simple, precisely balanced sentences to explain how he ended up in a Nazi concentration camp during World War II:

> In Germany, the Nazis first came for the Communists, and I didn't speak up because I wasn't a Communist. Then they came for the Jews, and I didn't speak up because I wasn't a Jew. Then they came for the trade unionists, and I didn't speak up because I wasn't a trade unionist. Then they came for the Catholics, and I didn't speak up because I was a Protestant. Then they came for me, and by that time there was no one left to speak for me.

Exercise   **4-5**

The following sentences were written by students whose grasp of parallel structure was less than perfect. I want you to restore the balance. Don't aim for impressive, emphatic sentences in this exercise. Just try to produce good, clear, everyday sentences.

First, read each sentence and decide which parts need to be parallel. Look for elements in series and phrases or clauses connected by coordinating conjunctions (*and*, *but*, *or*, *for*, *nor*, *yet*, *so*). Then, change the part that's irregular so that its grammatical structure matches the structure of the coordinate parts. Often you can find several ways to improve each sentence, each way equally good. I'll do one first to show you the technique.

1   The plan is not workable; it delegates a dangerous amount of power to
the government, and because it is unconstitutional.

That sentence consists of three clauses in series. All three should be
parallel. The first two are both independent clauses (subjects are underlined once, verbs twice):

>   The plan is not workable
>
>   it delegates a dangerous amount of power to the government

Fine so far. The clauses don't have to be precisely parallel as long as the
basic pattern (in this case, subject-verb-complement) is the same. The
trouble comes with the third clause, which is not independent but dependent (beginning with the subordinating conjunction *because*):

>   because it is unconstitutional.

Probably the easiest way to revise the sentence is to make all three clauses
independent by dropping the subordinating word *because*:

>   *Revised:*   The plan is not workable; it delegates a dangerous
>   amount of power to the government, and it is uncon-
>   stitutional.

You could also make both the second and third clauses dependent by
adding another *because*, like this:

>   *Revised:*   The plan is not workable because it delegates a
>   dangerous amount of power to the government and
>   because it is unconstitutional.

2   The first part of the Bus Stop, a disco dance, consists of three steps
backwards, a touch step, and then stepping forward three times.

3   The dancer should remember to act unruffled, self-composed, and as
though the steps came naturally.

4   After the dancer repeats the first part, a sideways two-step is executed,
and the dancer then two-steps back into the starting position.

5   Experienced dancers say that the hops and touches in the third part of the
Bus Stop are the most exciting and also hard to teach to others.

6   The final step is executing a ninety-degree kick-turn and to start the pattern
over from the beginning.

7   European trains are frequent, punctual, provide easy connections, and travel at high speeds.

8   In the movies all college men are portrayed as single and having other attributes such as money, good looks, and a great personality.

9   You have never heard so many joyous cries and laughter in your life.

10   Progressive education aims to teach children to be open-minded, logical-thinking, collecting evidence to make wise choices, self-discipline, and self-control.

11   This caused me to return home with a feeling of being a number in his appointment schedule and that there are other numbers just like me every day.

12   I feel quite uneasy when a commercial comes on about feminine hygiene spray or have Jane Russell come out and tell me she can't believe she's got a girdle on.

STRAIGHTENING OUT SCREWED-UP SENTENCES: MIXED CONSTRUCTIONS

Some sentence errors are impossible to categorize as anything other than messed up. And they are the worst kind because they make no sense. These semantic disasters are sometimes called—for lack of a better term—*mixed constructions*. They apparently result when the writer begins to say something one way, loses track in the middle, and finishes another way. That's a guess anyway. Heaven only knows how they actually happen because the students who write them are more surprised than anybody when confronted with these prodigies. These are the kinds of sentences that make readers do a double take—we shake our heads, rub our eyes, and read them again, hoping for a better connection next time. But we never get it from mix-ups like these:

> When students have no time for study or moral training also breeds a decadent society.

> The first planned crime will tell how well a boy has learned whether or not he is caught to become a juvenile delinquent.

Now those are pretty hopeless cases. They need to be scrapped. You'll lose more time trying to patch up a troublesome sentence than you will by backing off and beginning a different way. Take that last example. It needs a totally different beginning:

> Whether or not he is caught in his first planned crime may determine whether a boy will become a juvenile delinquent.

Occasionally a screwed-up sentence can be easily revised, like this one:

> When frequently opening and closing the oven door, it can cause a soufflé to fall.

All you need to do to correct that one is scratch out the *when*, the *it*, and the comma:

> Frequently opening and closing the oven door can cause a soufflé to fall.

These mixed constructions seem to reflect varying degrees of illiteracy, but I imagine they usually result from nothing but sheer, unpardonable carelessness. For this reason I beg you to proofread. And pay attention while you do it so that these linguistic misfortunes won't slip by you.

Exercise 4-6

Try to straighten out the following mixed constructions. Some of them cannot be easily patched up: you need to back off and begin in a different way. I will revise the first one.

1 Sherry, hoping to find a job that interests her, and so she doesn't have to type.

> *Revised:* Sherry is hoping to find a job that interests her—one that doesn't involve typing.

> *Revised:* Sherry is hoping to find an interesting job in which she doesn't have to type.

2 The Rites of Spring festival has been postponed because of too many students are sick with the flu.
3 Marijuana users should stop being made into criminals.
4 Only through constant study will achieve academic excellence.
5 In time of crisis must be handled with cool judgment.

Chapter 5

Work on Your Words

In order to produce first-rate writing, you need to revise each sentence—
to make it more clear perhaps, more vivid, more concise, more interesting, or more forceful. At the same time, you need to consider how
your audience may respond to your word choice. You want to make
sure that the terms you have chosen will be pleasing to your readers.

SELECT AN APPROPRIATE USAGE LEVEL

The nature of your audience and your purpose will determine whether
you should use slang or contractions or six-syllable words—that is,
your *level of usage*. The three main usage levels—*formal*, *informal*,
and *colloquial*—overlap considerably. You need different levels of
usage for different writing occasions, just as you sometimes need formal
and informal clothes, plus your grubbies for around the house. Good
usage is a matter of using language appropriate for the occasion. Figure
5-1 provides an illustration of these usage levels.

Figure 5-1 Usage levels for all occasions.

Formal:	One should not admit defeat too quickly.
	I shall not admit defeat too quickly.
Informal:	We should not give up too quickly.
	I'll not give up too quickly.
Colloquial:	I'm not going to throw in the towel too quick.
Nonstandard:	I ain't gonna throw in the towel, nohow.

Formal	Informal	Colloquial (slang)
automobile	car	wheels
comprehend	understand	dig
depart	leave	split
residence	house	pad
odious	offensive	gross
debilitated	exhausted	wasted
dejected	sad	down
hyperactive	jittery	wired
intoxicated	drunk	sloshed

Formal Writing

Formal writing is a lot less formal than it used to be. Many textbooks (not this one, though) are written in formal English, as are most scholarly articles and books and a few magazines. Most business communication still observes many of the rules of formal usage, but recently the use of *I* and *we* is replacing the strictly formal, third-person approach. Here are the main characteristics of formal usage:

1 No contractions
2 No slang
3 Third-person approach (*one*, *he*, *she*, *it*, *they*) (Do not address readers directly as *you*.)
4 No sentence fragments for emphasis (Look up *fragment* on page 202 if you don't know what one is.)
5 A serious or neutral tone

In order to get the feel of writing in the third person, try turning the sentences in the following exercise from first person into the more formal third. The more you practice writing in third person, the more natural—and thus effective—your use of it will become when your purpose requires it.

Exercise   **5-1**

The following sentences are written using the first person (*I* and *we*) and the informal second person (*you*). Rewrite each sentence to eliminate every *you*, as well as all slang and contractions. Try to use the formal third person (*one*, *she*, *he*, *it*, or *they*). But if the sentence sounds stilted, go back to *I* or *we*. The use of first person—especially *we*—is acceptable in much formal writing today. I'll show you how with the first one.

1   The point I want to make is quite simple.

    Revised: The point is quite simple.
    Revised: The point one wants to make is quite simple.

2   We hold these truths to be self-evident.
3   We must suppose, then, that the figures cited are OK.
4   You should eat nutritious foods if you want to stay healthy.
5   You can't help expressing yourself, unless you live in a vacuum.
6   If you would hold the attention of your readers, you should cultivate a pleasing style.
7   We shouldn't make editorial decisions solely upon our personal likes and dislikes.
8   The very people who most try your patience are often those who want to please you.
9   If you attain high office, your responsibility to other people increases.
10 We often find ourselves unable to resist temptation.

Informal Writing

The bulk of the writing you'll be called upon to do will probably be *informal*, which means ordinary, familiar, everyday writing. Here are the guidelines for informal usage:

1   You can use contractions, if you want to.
2   Use slang *only* if appropriate for your audience.

3 Write in the first person; address your readers as *you*, if you wish.
4 You may use an occasional sentence fragment—as long as each fragment is stylistically effective.
5 Adopt any tone appropriate for the audience and the purpose.

Colloquial Writing

In colloquial writing you have a lot of leeway, since *colloquial* means the language of the everyday speech of educated people. There's not much call for colloquial writing, of course, but it comes in handy for reproducing the flavor of a person's actual speech in an essay that is otherwise informal. Be careful if you decide to use colloquial language because your readers may be annoyed if they feel such extreme informality is not suitable for the subject under discussion. Remember also that usage levels are seldom pure, except perhaps for the formal. This textbook, for instance, is written on an informal level but occasionally has touches of the colloquial. Here are the characteristics of colloquial writing:

1 Contractions are expected.
2 Slang is fine.
3 First person and second person (*I* and *you*) are typical.
4 Sentence fragments are characteristic.
5 Tone is light, often humorous.

Nonstandard Usage

Since *standard usage* means the language used by educated people, *nonstandard usage* means any language (like *he don't*) that fails to conform to the accepted standard. (This textbook, by the way, offers advice on standard usage.) Unfortunately, dialectical expressions are considered nonstandard. Some dictionaries even label nonstandard constructions *illiterate*, which seems harsh, but you should be advised that many people are unalterably prejudiced against nonstandard English. Avoid it in writing, or use it only with extreme caution for stylistic effect.

Writing Exercise   5-2

Compose a brief paragraph in which you try to persuade a group of your peers that they should conserve electricity or gasoline or natural gas. Then rewrite the paragraph twice more, choosing a suitable usage level to address each of the groups below. Be prepared to explain the differences in your three versions.

1   The Lost Souls Motorcycle Club
2   The Presbyterian Ladies' Missionary Society

AVOID SEXIST LANGUAGE

In considering your audience, keep in mind that many of your readers may be displeased by sexist language. The word *sexist* (coined by analogy with the word *racist*) means stereotyping females and males according to traditional sex roles.

Our language reflects a sex bias that is ingrained in our society. Since it's awkward to repeatedly say *he or she*, *his or hers*, or *him or her*, it was long ago decreed by an act of the British Parliament that *he*, *his*, and *him* would refer to both sexes. That probably doesn't even sound unfair, unless you're female—or unless you've encountered William F. Buckley's extension of this principle. Mr. Buckley assures us that "the phrase 'will appeal to adventure-loving boys' is not an exclusionary phrase because the word 'boys' in this case means not only boys but also girls."[1] Now, everyone can at once see the injustice of that assertion because we're not accustomed to having the word *boys* mean *girls*.

Feminists would like for people to get *un*accustomed to accepting male orientation in language. Probably the easiest way to achieve non-sexist pronoun reference is to write whenever possible in the plural. We have perfectly neutral plural pronouns: *they/their/them*. Dr. Spock in his best-selling baby book no longer refers throughout to the *mother/she*, but to the *parents/they*. He even goes one step further: When he can't avoid using *baby* in the singular, he no longer says the *baby/he* but rather, the *baby/she*. If this reversal seems too daring, go ahead and use an occasional "his or her." The double pronoun has now become standard usage and really isn't cumbersome—as long as you don't overdo it.

[1]William F. Buckley, "Give the Lady an Inch," Bloomington *Daily Pantagraph*, July 13, 1974, Sec. 1, p. 4, col. 4.

REMEMBER: **If you can write what you want to say just as well in the plural, the problem won't even come up.**

For more information on avoiding sexist language, see the entries for *he or she*, *man/person*, and *Ms.* in Chapter 7, "Glossary of Usage."

Exercise   **5-3**

See if you can eliminate all the sexist language from the following sentences without changing the meaning or causing awkwardness. I'll work out the first one for you.

1 Man must work in order to eat.

    Revised: One must work in order to eat.
               People must work in order to eat.

2 Anyone with a brain in his head can see the dangers of utilizing atomic reactors.
3 The citizen may pay his water bill by mail or at city hall.
4 The gregarious dog is man's best friend, but the more aloof cat keeps his own counsel.
5 He who laughs last laughs best.
6 "As long as man is on earth, he's likely to cause problems. But the man at General Electric will keep trying to find answers." (advertisement for GE)
7 Clyde was patched up by a lady doctor who stopped her car at the accident scene.
8 Gertie's mother is a computer repairman at IBM.
9 The hippopotamus is happiest when he is half submerged in mud.
10 The American pioneers loaded their wagons and moved their wives and children westward.

BE WARY OF EUPHEMISMS

While considering word choice, you should give a fleeting thought to the sensibilities of your readers. If they have led a sheltered life, you may want to soften your language when saying something unpleasant, unpopular, or sexy. You can employ linguistic smokescreens called *euphemisms*, most of which are quite innocent. Rather than say bluntly, ''He died of cancer,'' you can say, ''He passed away after a lingering illness.'' It takes the shudder out and cloaks the whole grim business of dying in a soothing phrase. Undertakers (or ''funeral directors,'' as they prefer to be called) sometimes carry euphemism to grotesque extremes, like calling the room where the body lies the ''slumber chamber.'' And my dear little Victorian mother quaintly used to refer to the ''white meat'' of the chicken (instead of the ''breast'') and to the ''second joint'' (instead of the ''thigh'').

Such delicacy is amusing and does no harm, but some people also use a sinister kind of euphemism, called *doublespeak*, to mask realities that ought not be concealed. The CIA, for instance, substitutes the meaningless phrase ''to terminate with extreme prejudice'' for the blunt word ''murder.'' The Pentagon refers to weapons designed to kill human beings as ''antipersonnel implements'' and civilian casualties of a nuclear war are designated ''collateral damage.'' Instead of ''bombings,'' the Air Force announces ''protective reaction strikes.'' Such transparent attempts to make human slaughter sound inoffensive are far from innocent.

This deceptive misuse of language is becoming widespread in our society. Police officers are no longer taught to aim to kill. Now they aim ''to neutralize the adversary.'' The nuclear power industry refers to an accident as an ''abnormal evolution,'' speaks of a fire as a ''rapid oxidation,'' and calls an explosion an ''energetic disassembly.'' Such euphemisms are deliberately misleading and border on being immoral.

You need to decide according to the nature of your audience whether innocent euphemisms are appropriate or not. Certainly you should never use deceptive ones. Be honest both in what you say and in the way you say it.

BE CAUTIOUS ABOUT PROFANITY AND SLANG

There remains the question of whether to use yet another kind of euphemism. Many people consider it euphemistic to substitute more socially acceptable terms for our frank and forceful four-letter words. You should, again, consider your readers. You don't want to put them off; you want to communicate with them. Different people are shocked by different things, but all of us are offended by something. To some people violence is the ultimate obscenity. To some the sight or sound of four-letter words is obscene. We could argue about whose concept of obscenity is valid and whose isn't, but that wouldn't necessarily help you avoid offending your readers. You'll need to size them up for yourself. Before you toss in four-letter words for emphasis, try to decide whether your readers will find them forceful or merely offensive. And when in doubt, leave them out.

A number of readers object also to the use of slang in writing—on any level, even informal. Slang terms like *nerd*, *wimp*, *woozy*, and *slammer* and phrases like *psyched up*, *shagged out*, and *down the tube* can be lively and descriptive, but F. L. Lucas, for instance, considers slang "a kind of linguistic fungus; as poisonous, and as short-lived as toadstools." Your dictionary will tell you if a word is slang; if you don't find it listed, you may assume that it is slang. Remember, you don't want to put your readers off; you want to communicate with them. Slang often is an in-group language known only to those of a certain age or ethnic background. As a matter of courtesy, you should never use slang that your readers won't understand or may find offensive.

CUT OUT UNNECESSARY WORDS

Try to make your writing clean, clear, and concise. I don't mean to deprive you of effective stylistic flourishes, but *ineffective* stylistic flourishes have got to go. So does just plain lazy wordiness. It's far easier to be verbose than it is to be concise. In *Provincial Letters*, *XVI* (1657), Pascal wrote, "I have made this letter longer than usual because I lack the time to make it shorter." And Hugh Henry Brackenridge in *Modern Chivalry* (1792) observed, "In order to speak short on any subject, think long." Nothing will annoy your readers more than having to waste time plowing through a cluttered paragraph because you neglected to spend your time cleaning it up.

You must be diligent and prune your prose. Sentences like the following cause any reader to contemplate justifiable homicide:

It is believed by a number of persons in this country that the young people of today do not assume as much responsibility toward society as it might be hoped that they would.   (33 words)

You can say the same thing better with fewer words:

Today many people believe that our young people assume too little responsibility toward society.   (14 words)

Notice, for instance, that *at this point in time* means exactly the same thing as *at this point. During this period of time* means the same as *during this time.* Spare your readers the unnecessary words.

Exercise   **5-4**

Sharpen your editing skills by tidying the following littered sentences. Try to keep the same meaning but eliminate all unnecessary wordiness. I will show you how with the first one.

1   It has been in the most recent past that many different groups of citizens have joined together in completely unanimous protest against the concept of nuclear war.

    Revised: Recently many groups have joined in unanimous protest against nuclear war.

2   It is my desire to be called Ishmael.
3   There is a general consensus that the paper which is judged to be the most original should be awarded the prize.
4   By and large a stitch sewed or basted as soon as a rip is discovered may well save nine times the amount of sewing necessary if the job is put off even for a short time.
5   At future meetings, please do not request an exemption from being present at the meeting.
6   We finally selected a desk that was small in size and grey in color.
7   The participants who engage in polo playing seem to be few in number.
8   It is absolutely essential that we do something about the complete absence of members of minority groups among the members of this important committee.
9   The reason that I think we should postpone our decision on this problem is because this problem is a complex matter.

10   There was a feeling, at least on my part, based upon a number of true
      facts that I had been reading, that the food that we buy at the supermarket
      to eat may be poisoned with food additives.

Use Repetition Wisely

Deliberate repetition, such as you observed in those impressive,
balanced sentences in the previous chapter, can be one of your most
effective rhetorical devices. But *careless repetition* may offend your
readers as much as wordiness. Ineffective repetition is often the result
of thoughtlessness, as in this student's sentence:

> Walking up to the door, I came upon the skeleton head of a cow
> placed next to the door.

That's too many *to the door* phrases. Just changing the first phrase
solves the problem:

> Walking up to the house, I came upon the skeleton head of a cow
> placed next to the door.

You need to eliminate any word or phrase that's been carelessly used
twice.

Effective repetition is an entirely different matter. You can achieve
both clarity and emphasis by repeating a key term deliberately, as
Katherine Anne Porter does in this sentence describing the execution
of Sacco and Vanzetti (my italics):

> They were put to death in the electric chair at Charlestown Prison at
> *midnight* on the 23rd of August, 1927, a desolate dark *midnight*, a *night* for
> perpetual remembrance and mourning.

Just be sure the word deserves the emphasis before you purposely repeat
yourself.

BE SPECIFIC AND VIVID AND CLEAR

Paul Roberts once wrote that most subjects—except sex—are basically
boring, so it's up to the writer to make the topic interesting. Since you

can't write about sex *all* the time, you need to incorporate some of the following suggestions aimed at keeping your readers awake.

Choose Lively Words

One way to liven up your sentences (and hence your writing) is to use lively, specific words whenever possible. You can't avoid the limp *to be* verb (*am, was, been, is, are, were,* etc.) a great deal of the time, but given a chance, toss in a forceful verb. James Thurber, in his essay "Sex Ex Machina," speaks of a "world made up of gadgets that *whir* and *whine* and *whiz* and *shriek* and sometimes *explode.*" (Italics mine.) The force of the verbs conveys the feeling of anxiety produced by machine-age living. In his essay "A Hanging," George Orwell describes a dog that "came *bounding* among us with a loud volley of barks, and *leapt* round us *wagging* its whole body, wild with glee at finding so many human beings together." (Italics mine.) The verb *leapt*, plus the italicized verbal adjectives, here enable the reader to visualize the energy and excitement of the dog. Thomas Heggen, in the introduction to *Mr. Roberts*, writes, "Surely an artillery shell fired at Hanover *ripples* the air here. Surely a bomb dropped on Okinawa *trembles* these bulkheads." (Italics mine.) These verbs produce precisely the effect he wants in the two sentences: the suggestion of being touched, but only barely touched, by events far away.

There are, of course, other stylistic elements combining to make the above examples effective. But if your writing is colorless and tiresome, you may need to practice using lively verbs and specific details. Instead of writing, "We got into the car," try "All four of us piled into Herman's Honda." You can, of course, overdo the use of forceful verbs and specifics, but most of us err in the other direction and our writing comes out flat.

Exercise 5-5

In order to limber up your imagination, try rewriting the following dull sentences, substituting vivid, precise words for any general or lackluster terms. I'll do the first one to give you an example.

1 Seymour was up late last night trying to finish typing his term paper.

Revised: Seymour sat hunched over his typewriter, pecking away doggedly until three o'clock in the morning, trying to finish his paper on the mating habits of hippopotamuses.

2 My friend, who exercises as a hobby, studies at night in order to have his afternoons free for sports.
3 That cat is behaving in a most peculiar fashion.
4 Some person had removed the very article I needed from the magazine in the library.
5 She came into the room, removed her shoes, and sat down.
6 Hearing someone make even slight noises at a symphony is distracting.
7 The woman left her office, walked hurriedly to the store, and made a purchase.
8 The man (woman) I went out with last night was a real character.
9 Clyde and I have just been out driving around in his new car.
10 Near the window was an attractive plant in an interesting container.

FIND THE EXACT WORD

Mark Twain once observed that the difference between the right word and almost the right word is the difference between the lightning and the lightning bug. Our language is full of synonyms; but synonyms have different shades of meaning. Although a *feeling* is a *sensation*, the two words are not interchangeable. A pen is not a writing *utensil*; it's a writing *implement* or *instrument*. And *uninterested* does not mean the same thing as *disinterested*.

Dust off Your Dictionary

Any good desk-size dictionary can enlighten you on these distinctions if you'll take the trouble to look the words up. But in order to get reliable help from your dictionary, you should first learn how to use it. For some reason, myths abound concerning dictionaries. Many people believe that the first meaning listed for a word is the "best" one. Not true. There is no "best" one. The first meaning will often be the oldest meaning; hence, it could be the least common one. The same thing is true of alternative spellings. Unless some qualifier is inserted (like "also" or "variation of"), multiple spelling listings are equally acceptable.

The only way to find out how your dictionary handles these matters is to force yourself to read the ''Explanatory Notes'' at the beginning. It's not the liveliest reading imaginable, but it can be rewarding. You'll find out, for instance, that in most dictionaries the principal parts of verbs, degrees of adjectives, and plurals of nouns are not listed unless irregular. You'll find, if you persevere, explanations of various usage labels, which warn you about words with limited uses (archaic, slang, substandard, etc.). You may also, if you have an inquiring mind, discover interesting material in the back that you never suspected was there: many dictionaries include lists of abbreviations, proofreader's marks, signs, and symbols; rules for spelling, punctuation, and capitalization; and sometimes a list of all the colleges and universities in the United States and Canada. A good college dictionary is something you will use often if you write well. If the only thing you ever do with your dictionary is use it to prop up other books, that may be part of your problem.

Trot out Your Thesaurus

A pocket-size thesaurus (dictionary of synonyms) comes in handy for locating just the right word. If you need a synonym for a word, either because you think it's not the precise word or because you've used it three times already, locate that word in your thesaurus just as you would in a dictionary. Instead of a definition, you'll find a handsome selection of words with related meanings. Remember, though, that synonyms aren't always interchangeable. Never choose an unfamiliar word unless you first look it up in the dictionary to make sure it conveys the exact meaning you want.

Increase Your Vocabulary

The only safe, sure way to increase your vocabulary is to take note of new words as you encounter them in reading, in the classroom, in conversation, in movies—in other words, as they appear in context. If you become conscious of new words, you'll start absorbing them almost by osmosis. I have used in this book a number of words that I wouldn't expect a college freshman to understand in hopes that you might take a fancy to some and look them up. You'll encounter them again and they'll be familiar next time. Before long, you'll be using them in your own writing—and using them correctly.

SAY WHAT YOU MEAN

Sometimes a sentence comes out as nonsense not because the writer confuses unusual words but because the person somehow fails to pay attention to what common words mean. The following sentences *sound* all right—until you think about them. A police officer recently announced in the local paper:

> We are trying to put some teeth into the law to help enforce narcotics abuse.

We can hope he doesn't really intend to force everyone to abuse narcotics. More likely he meant "to help *curb* narcotics abuse," but he actually *said* he intended to make drug abuse mandatory. A student confidently made this observation in an essay:

> Many important factors are determined by the way one dresses: the person's personality, lifestyle, profession, age, and sex.

She couldn't seriously believe that changing one's manner of dress could also change one's "profession, age, and sex," but that's what she *said*. Another student wrote this puzzler:

> Some wives have to hold jobs to help support the family's low income.

That is a grammatically correct but confusing sentence. The student meant "to help *supplement* the family's low income"—or else simply, "to help support the family."

Some people mix up words that sound alike—which confuses readers who know what the words actually mean. If you write, "Tighten all the lose screws," people may think *you* have a screw loose. Consult Chapter 9, the "Glossary of Usage," if you are in doubt about whether to write *effect* or *affect*, *lie* or *lay*, or any of those other words that are hard to keep straight.

When you write, pay attention to the words you choose. When you revise, study your word choice again. Be sure that each sentence is perfectly clear and means exactly what you want to say. Try also to make sure that you have said it in the best possible words.

Exercise   5-6

The following sentences—all taken from actual usage—employ words
without regard for meaning. First, point out what's wrong with each
one, and then rephrase it accurately. You may need to revise some
extensively in order to repair them. I'll rewrite the first one, which
appeared on a sign in a parking lot.

1 Illegal Parking Will Be Towed Away At Their Expense.

   Revised: Illegally Parked Cars Will Be Towed at Owners' Expense.

2 Because she was disinterested in the novel, she called it "boring."
3 Despite the enormous number of books in the world, it is possible to
   generalize them into three categories.
4 My brother confides in me not to tell on him.
5 Today's society has been pilfered with a barrage of illegal drugs.
6 These figures deduce that the firm could expect a loss.
7 I have apprised the situation and find it perilous.
8 But I am going irregardless of what you say.
9 There are a variety of media under the classification of painting.
10 Myself and Officer Smith responded to the eighth floor by way of the
   stairwell.

Avoid Jargon and Clichés

As you search for the right word, be careful about words that may
sound grand but have vague meanings. Avoid elevated language if you
can say the same thing clearly and plainly without it.

Jargon usually means pretentious language used by people to make
themselves sound smarter than anybody else. Such language is always
ineffective because it sets up a barrier to communication. Jargon can
also refer to language used within a trade or profession which is understood perfectly well among that specialized group but not among
outsiders. Bridge players mean something entire different by *rubber*,
dummy, and *slam* than the rest of us do.

Consider your audience and your purpose. If your readers are all
familiar with the jargon, use it—provided it's the best way to make

your meaning clear. But the kind of jargon you should try to avoid includes those monstrous new words that creep into the language via the federal bureaucracy, the educational establishment, and the social sciences—phrases like "increased propensity to actualize" (meaning "apt to occur"); "facilitate the availability of funds" (meaning "to help get money"); and "sociologically compatible behavioral parameters" (meaning who knows what).

Clichés are phrases we pick up because they sound good, but then we use them over and over until they lose their force and become annoying. Some *old chestnuts* are *cool as a cucumber*, *ship of state*, *rugged individualist*, and *frontiers of knowledge*. The simple word *fine* is preferable to the tarnished phrase *worth its weight in gold*. Here is a list of currently popular clichés that you may be tempted to use. Try to resist the temptation.

acid test	doomed to failure	interface with
at this point	few and far between	in this day and age
in time	first and foremost	last but not least
ball park figure	for all intents and	paid my dues
bottom line	purposes	pretty as a picture
burning questions	have a nice day	state of the art
crystal clear	history tells us	untimely death
crucial test	high and mighty	user-friendly
cutting edge	high tech	

USE YOUR IMAGINATION

Try to come up with at least a few lively *figures of speech*—analogies, metaphors, similes—to give zest to your writing. If you set your imagination loose, you'll be able to come up with imaginative comparisons that will give your writing greater interest and clarity. Ralph Waldo Emerson once remarked that "New York is a sucked orange." Now that's an observation full of insight, phrased with great economy. Maya Angelou, speaking of the struggle for civil rights, mentions that some changes "have been as violent as electrical storms, while others creep slowly like sorghum syrup." Such comparisons are a form of *analogy*, a useful method of comparing something abstract (like the quality of life in a city) to something concrete (like a sucked orange). Here's a simple but effective analogy from J. F. Kobler: "Like really good tomatoes, performance standards in each department must be home grown."

When Dorothy Parker declares, "His voice was as intimate as the rustle of sheets," she lets us know that the man was speaking seductively. Certainly her *simile*—an imaginative comparison stated with *like* or *as*—is more interesting than just telling us so. Notice how forcefully Barbara Ehrenreich conveys the hazards of smoking when she asserts that the "medical case against smoking is as airtight as a steel casket." Brigid Brophy uses a *metaphor*—an implied or suggested imaginative comparison—to assert her belief that monogamy is a confining relationship: "At present, monogamy is the corset into which we try to fit every married couple—a process which has on so many occasions split the seams that we have had to modify the corset."

The only thing you need to be wary about is the *mixed metaphor*—the comparison that doesn't compare accurately, like this choice one from the *Nashville Tennessean:* "I may be just a little grain of salt crying in the woods, but I deplore this kind of thing." Just try to visualize that image and you'll see why it's a mistake. Better no metaphor at all than one that's confused.

Most importantly: Remember that *figures of speech should clarify your meaning* through comparisons that increase your readers' understanding.

Exercise   **5-7**

If writing analogies doesn't come naturally to you, try practicing by filling in the blanks to finish these comparisons:

1 Kissing my lover is like _____ .
2 Failing an exam is like _____ .
3 Eating in the cafeteria is like _____ .
4 Going to the health service is like _____ .
5 Getting busted is like _____ .
6 Losing a lover is like _____ .
7 My room looks like _____ .
8 Falling in love is like _____ .

9   Writing a theme for English class is like _____ .
10   Washing the dog is like _____ .

REVISING THE WHOLE (IF YOU SKIP THIS STAGE, I CAN'T HELP YOU)

When you've finally completed your rough draft, you'll feel elated, as if the task is finally done. And indeed, you are practically through. But many students at this point rush the manuscript to a typist—either a professional one or a handy, inexpensive one located on the premises. Don't do it. Not without some further revising.

If you haven't yet hit on a good introduction or conclusion, you must now apply yourself to that task—with or without inspiration. You'll need a title, too. For advice, look up *Title Tactics*, Chapter 8, the alphabetized "Revising Index." Now is a good time also to look up word meanings in doubtful cases and to check your thesaurus if necessary.

Also, pay attention as you reread the paper to be sure your paragraphs are fully developed with clear transitions between ideas. Be sure that you haven't strayed from your outline and taken any little side trips with only a passing relationship to your thesis.

Most important of all, be sure that the whole makes sense—that each sentence is clear, not just to you but to anyone who chances to read the paper. Be sure that each sentence *is* a sentence, not a fragment, unless you have used a fragment deliberately for stylistic purposes.

Cajole a Loved One into Reading It

Finally, try to talk someone else into reading your paper—and not just for spelling, punctuation, and typographical errors. Ask your benefactor to call your attention to any sentences that don't make sense, any points that aren't clear. Then rework those sentences; add illustrations to clarify the weak points. You may have to rewrite a page or two, but do it, and try to be grateful for having caught the problems before instead of after turning in the paper. Most humane teachers will overlook a typo or a minor spelling error, but few will forgive a breach in communication. And rightly so. Work hard to make your content clear. Try also to make it graceful, make it persuasive, make it forceful. But primarily make it communicate, and you will have fulfilled your chief obligation as a writer.

Following is a revising checklist that will help you (as you go over your draft yet one more time) make sure you have given your work the proper polish.

Revising Checklist

In order to make this piece of writing a paper to be proud of, be sure that your

1 Thesis involves an idea worth developing.
2 Level of usage is appropriate for your audience.
3 Language is not sexist, profane, or unduly slangy.
4 Introduction makes the point of the paper clear and catches the readers' interest.
5 Ideas are logically arranged and easy to follow.
6 Ideas are completely clear throughout.
7 Paragraphs contain plenty of examples.
8 Sentences are well constructed and precisely worded.
9 Conclusion makes or reinforces the point of your thesis.
10 Final sentence is pleasing, maybe even emphatic.

PROOFREAD THE FINAL DRAFT

Even after you've typed or printed out a clean copy, you must force yourself (or someone completely trustworthy) to read the paper once more to pick up assorted minor mistakes that didn't show up in the rough draft but will glare like neon signs in the final draft. Jessica Mitford rightly says that "failure to proofread is like preparing a magnificent dinner and forgetting to set the table, so that the wretched guests have to scramble for the food as best they can." So, be polite: proofread.

Careless errors can be funny and Freudian, like this one from a student discussing public reaction to the changing morality of the twenties: "Ladies' skirts finally rose so high that the public was shocked." But careless errors can also be witless and annoying—like repeating a word needlessly ("and and") or leaving off an *s* and producing an illiteracy: "The protester were arrested and herded off to

jail.'' Such errors do nothing to encourage the readers' admiration for
the brilliance of your observations—no matter how keen they are. So
watch the little things, too. Don't write "probable" for "probably,"
or "use to" for "used to," or "you" for "your," or "then" for
"than." Check possessives to be sure the apostrophes are there—or
not there in the case of *its*. You'll momentarily confuse your readers
if you get that one wrong. (If you are at all in doubt about the distinction between *its* and *it's*, consult Chapter 9, the "Glossary of Usage.")

Proofreading and Editing Checklist

Reread the paper one more time *paying no attention to content* but
checking to be sure that

1 No words are left out or carelessly repeated.
2 No words are misspelled (or carelessly spelled—*use to* for *used to*).
3 No plurals are left off.
4 No apostrophes are omitted (for possessives or contractions).
5 No periods, dashes, commas, colons, or quotation marks are left
out.

Make the necessary corrections. If you're using a word processor, this
step will take only a matter of minutes. Remember, a handsomely typed
paper has a psychological advantage. It suggests to your readers that
time and effort went into the preparation, that it wasn't tossed off at
the last minute. If you're typing, make corrections neatly in black ink
above the line, and retype any page that looks like it's ready for urban
renewal.

Chapter 6

Smart Reading and
Straight Thinking

Just as important as the writing process is the reading process that transmits the ideas into your head. The writing you do in college and thereafter will probably demand that you go beyond relating personal experiences as such. You'll find it necessary to write about issues and events—to deal with ideas, theories, and opinions as well as facts. And you'll be continually reading in order to acquire informed ideas of your own on various subjects. Reading, discussing, synthesizing all this new information constitutes a large part of becoming educated.

CULTIVATE A QUESTIONING ATTITUDE

But the educational process bogs down unless you keep an open mind. You shouldn't reject a new idea just because it conflicts with an opinion you presently treasure. Because you've heard and accepted a statement all your life doesn't make that statement true. As Mark Twain observed, in his *Notebook*, "One of the proofs of immortality is that myriads have believed it. They also believed that the world was flat." You should be willing to consider new ideas, examine them, think about them, and decide on the basis of the available evidence what is and is not valid. You'll be bombarded by facts and opinions from all sides. In self-defense you must try to distinguish the truth from the tripe. It's not easy. Truth may be mighty, but it doesn't always prevail.

DEFINE YOUR TERMS

Most of our abstract words mean slightly different things to different people. Some of them mean entirely different things, depending on the point of view. "Individual freedom," for instance, means to some people the absence of governmental control in business, i.e., the freedom to pursue profits without restraint. To other people, though, "individual freedom" means the liberty to read whatever they wish, to see any movies they find interesting, to make love to any person of either sex in any manner agreeable to all: that is, strictly personal freedom. Virtually all terms dealing with morality and ethics need to be clarified.

If one of those slippery, abstract terms figures importantly in your writing, you should probably define it. Usually a brief, dictionary-type definition is all you need, like the one Gore Vidal provides here:

> Put simply, fascism is the control of the state by a single man or by an oligarchy, supported by the military and the police. That is why I keep emphasizing the dangers of corrupt police forces, of uncontrolled *secret* police, like the F.B.I. and the C.I.A. and Army counterintelligence and the Treasury men— what a lot of sneaky types we have spying on us all!

> —"The State of the Union,"
> *Esquire* (May 1975)

You may consider his charge exaggerated, but his tactic of defining the term *fascism* encourages us at least to examine the possibility that what he says may be true. Notice also the ease with which he inserts his definition: "Put simply, fascism is. . . ." That's much more graceful than "According to the dictionary . . ." or (shudder) "Webster says. . . ." You should, of course, consult the dictionary, but then define the terms in your own words, making your definition parallel in form (i.e., same part of speech or same verb tense as the word defined).

BE SUSPICIOUS OF SLOGANS

As you form the habit of questioning statements, the first ones to examine are the ones that come in the form of epigrams or slogans. These prepackaged ideas are all neat and tidy, easy to remember, pleasant to the ear. We've been brought up on them and have Ben Franklin to thank for a sizable number, like "A stitch in time saves nine," and "Early to bed and early to rise makes a man healthy, wealthy, and wise." *Epigrams* usually state a simple truth, but often they cleverly disguise opinion as fact. For instance, we've always heard that "home is where the heart is," yet George Bernard Shaw says, "Home is the girl's prison and the woman's workhouse." Clearly, the absolute truth of either statement is debatable. In my opinion, Shaw's version has more of the ring of reality.

A *slogan* is a catchword or motto designed to rally people to vote for a certain party, agree with the opinions of a particular group, or buy a specific product. Bumper stickers reading "America—love it or leave it" or "America—change it or lose it" may inspire you, but don't mistake them for reasoned arguments. Your job as reader is to question such statements: Demand evidence and decide rationally rather than emotionally which opinions are valid, which are propaganda, which are a mixture of both.

BE CAUTIOUS ABOUT CONNOTATIONS

More difficult to perceive than the bias of slogans is the subtle persuasion of slanted writing. But once you become aware of the emotional quality of many words, you'll not likely be taken in by slanted writing.

Words are symbols with *denotative* meanings (the actual concrete property or abstract quality referred to) and *connotative* meanings (the emotional responses stimulated by associations with the word). The term *mother*, for instance, *denotes* the woman who gives birth to a child, but the term often *connotes* warmth, love, security, comfort. Most of our words have connotations in varying degrees—some so strong that the words should be considered "loaded." Whether you choose to refer to the President as a "statesman" or a "politician" may well reveal your political affiliation. Consider the connotations of these pairs of similar words:

smut	pornography
mob	gathering
cur	pup
smog	haze
egghead	intellectual
prudish	chaste
jock	athlete
penny-pinching	thrifty
foolhardy	courageous

Your attitude will be fairly transparently revealed by whether you choose from the strongly negative words on the left or the more favorable words on the right.

Consider, for example, Frederick Lewis Allen's description of Woodrow Wilson as a "Puritan Schoolmaster. . . . cool in a time of great emotions, calmly setting the lesson for the day; the moral idealist . . . , the dogmatic prophet of democracy. . . ." The word *Puritan* suggests a moralist devoid of human warmth. Allen could have said "high-minded" and lessened the chill factor. And what does the word *schoolmaster* suggest that the neutral word *teacher* does not? Again, a strict, no-nonsense, unsmiling disciplinarian. The word *cool* reinforces this same feeling, as does *calmly*. The term *moral idealist* should be totally complimentary. But is it? We associate idealists with good intentions, but a tinge of daydreaming impracticality clings to the word. *Dogmatic* denotes closed-mindedness. And *prophet* suggests an aura of fanaticism, since the Biblical prophets were always exhorting the fun-loving Old Testament sinners to repent of their evil ways or face the wrath of Jehovah. Allen has told us perhaps more through connotation in the sentence than he did through denotation. He slants the writing to convey a picture of Wilson that he feels is accurate—the image of a cold, determined, perhaps misguided man with the best of intentions.

Thus you shouldn't get the impression that connotative language is necessarily bad. It isn't. In fact, without the use of emotional words, writing would be virtually lifeless. But you must be *aware* of connotations, both as you read and as you write. The rhetoric in the following passage by Theodore Roosevelt is first-rate. The utterance has impact, conviction, persuasion. See if you can detect how much connotative words lend to the writer's effect:

If we stand idly by, if we seek merely swollen, slothful ease and ignoble peace . . . , then bolder and stronger peoples will pass us by, and will win for themselves the domination of the world.

Note that he says not "stand by" but "stand *idly* by." He fears we may seek "ease"—but not the ease that brings rest after wearying toil; instead, "*swollen, slothful* ease." Certainly the word *peace* alone would not serve: it is "*ignoble* peace." Notice, too, that the peoples who are going to "pass us by" and leave us with no world to dominate are "*bolder* and *stronger* peoples": we're subtly asked to envision not Turks and Visigoths slaughtering innocent hordes, but rather to picture clean-limbed, fearless types pressing onward against obstacles, propelled by what is presented as an admirable vision of world conquest. Surely the piece deserves high marks as effective propaganda. But you as reader must be able to detect that the chinks in his logic are effectively plugged with rhetoric. Your best protection from propaganda is your ability to think—to examine the language and the logic, to sort the soundness from the sound effects.

CONSIDER THE SOURCE

You could be reasonably sure, even before reading it, that you wouldn't get an unbiased comment from Theodore Roosevelt concerning the Spanish-American War. This doesn't mean, however, that you should ignore Roosevelt's statement if you're writing an appraisal of the reasons the United States entered that war. Neither should you ignore the opinions of William Jennings Bryan or H. L. Mencken if you're analyzing the fairness of the Scopes trial. But you should be constantly aware that the sources you're reading could hardly be considered impartial.

You might expect an unprejudiced analysis of an event from journalists who were present, but here again you must stay alert because not all publications achieve—or even *try* to achieve—objective reporting. You may be certain that the conservative *National Review* will offer an appreciably different appraisal from that of the ultraliberal *Mother Jones*. And the *Congressional Record*, which sounds like an unimpeachable source, is actually one of the least reliable, since any member of Congress can have any nonsense whatsoever read into the

Record. You must sample enough authorities so that you are able to weigh the matter and discount the prejudices. This is one reason that research papers require extensive bibliographies. You could probably scare up most of the facts from reading one *unbiased* source, but the problem is discovering which one—if any—that is. You'll have to read opinions on both sides of the middle in order to recognize the center— if and when you find it.

Don't make the mistake of embracing what you consider a reliable source and then placing your trust in it till death do you part. Too many of us do just this: we plight our troth to the Bible, to *The Nation*, to the *Wall Street Journal*, or to *Time* magazine, and assume we never have to think again. You will discover writers and publications whose viewpoint is similar to yours. These will naturally strike you as the most astute, cogent, perceptive, reliable sources to consult. But be careful that you don't fall into the comfortable habit of reading these publications exclusively.

The *date* of a publication often makes some difference in its value or reliability. If you're doing a paper analyzing the relative safety of legal and illegal abortions, you'll find an article written in 1936 of little use. If, on the other hand, you're writing a paper on the *history* of the long struggle to legalize abortion, a 1936 article could be quite important. In general, we place the highest value on recent articles simply because the latest scholar or scientist has the advantage of building on all that has gone before. Dr. Christiaan Barnard might never have been able to perform the first heart transplant had it not been for the pioneering genius of the seventeenth-century surgeon William Harvey, who first theorized the circulation of blood. But if you're writing about the effectiveness of heart transplants, your paper need not mention Harvey. Obviously, your data must be current to be of value in such an investigation.

Appealing to Authority

You're probably going to want to cite authorities whenever you write on any controversial subject. You can lose arguments, though, if your authority isn't convincing to your readers. Some people feel that once they've clinched a point with "The Bible says . . . ," they've precluded any rebuttal. If your reader happens to be Billy Graham or one of the faithful, you'll be on solid ground. But not everyone would agree with the upright citizen who offers this solution for helping the poor:

The only remedy against poverty is to worship God as God, honor His word and obey His doctrines, call upon Him and humble ourselves. Then He will hear and heal the land.[1]

The more practical-minded your readers, the less likely they will be to accept an argument requiring divine intervention to solve social problems.

You should cite authorities, by all means, but be sure they are recognized authorities on the subject you're considering. You might find some people who would value the opinion of the Pope on pornography, George Wallace on race relations, or Hugh Hefner on women's rights. But try for authorities who would come closer to being considered impartial experts on those subjects by the majority of reflective, educated people.

A QUICK LOOK AT LOGIC

Whenever you write using sources, your purpose is to convey your thoughts and ideas into the minds of your readers. But in order to be convincing, these thoughts and ideas must be logical. You should be aware of the common pitfalls of slippery logic so that you can avoid them in your own thinking and writing, as well as detect them in the arguments of others.

Avoid Oversimplifying

Most of us have a tendency to like things reduced to orderly, easily grasped *either/or* answers. The only problem is that things seldom are that simple. Be wary of arguments that offer only *either/or* choices, as if there exists no middle way—the "either we win the war, or we sacrifice our national honor" sort of reasoning. This fallacy is sometimes called the *false dichotomy*.

Stereotypes The same people who produce these alternatives will usually come up with *stereotypes* as well. They will be aware of only two types of students, for instance: the loud, rowdy, alcoholic hell-raisers; and the quiet, studious, well-mannered kids. Such stereotypes are based on the combination of a few facts and a lot of prejudice.

[1]Letter to the editor of the *Eugene* (Ore.) *Register-Guard*, September 18, 1969.

They seldom give a truthful picture of anyone in the group and could never be accurate to describe all the members.

Hasty Generalizations   You'll do well to question people who present easy solutions to complex problems. This ability to simplify could reflect genius, but more often it will stem from a lack of completely understanding the situation in the first place. Single-minded people, confident that they have all the answers, are always happy to enlighten you with what are called *hasty generalizations*, like this one:

> If the demonstrators had left when the police told them to, there would have been no trouble, and no one would have been killed.

The statement, which on the surface seems entirely plausible, conveys no force to anyone who doesn't share in the hidden premises (the underlying assumptions): that all the laws are just and are fairly administered; that all the actions of the government are honorable and in the best interest of all the citizens. The statement presumes, in short, that the demonstrators had no right or reason to be there and hence were entirely wrong not to leave when told to do so. Such a presumption overlooks the possibility that the demonstrators might legitimately protest the right of the state to silence their protests.

Oversimplification can also be achieved by merely stating opinions as facts. The Kansas lady who wrote the following letter to the editor of the *Wichita Eagle-Beacon* (June 17, 1965) has the technique down nicely:

> Liquor is something that we can get along without to a very good advantage. The problem of jazz music is a very grave one in this city, also, as it produces an attitude of irresponsibility in the listener. . . . The fact that it originates from undesirable heathen rituals should keep us from performing it.
>
> Let's keep Kansas attractive to God-fearing people. This is the type industry is interested in hiring and this is the type needed in government and the armed forces.

The letter is a study in logical fallacies. It's not necessary that you be able to distinguish them from one another. The name of the error isn't important: avoiding the error *is*.

Sweeping Generalizations

Since you can't avoid making general statements, you should be careful to avoid making them without sufficient evidence to support them. Suppose you write:

> All Siamese cats are extremely nervous creatures, far more jumpy than alley cats. My sister has a Siamese cat that will allow itself to be petted only with great hissing and trembling. But my striped tomcat is so friendly, he jumps up in the laps of complete strangers.

Personal experience is always convincing but you're not likely to prove to anyone's satisfaction that *all* Siamese cats are edgy by describing the behavior of only one. Neither have you proved that alley cats are indeed friendly by trotting out one pushy tomcat. You must either draw on a much larger body of experience, or else you're going to need to qualify your assertion considerably. Statements involving *all*, *none*, *everything*, *nobody*, and *always* are tough to prove. You may so damage your readers' confidence by exaggerating your point that they won't accept even the smaller truth that you can support.

So tone it down. *Qualify* your statement. If you really have seen several high-strung Siamese, and if you know of at least three or four out-going alley cats, you might try saying it like this:

> Siamese cats are often aloof and edgy around strangers, but alley cats will sometimes be as friendly as a beagle pup.

Then you mention your experience with lots of cats, and your readers will be more likely to accept your generalization.

Jumping to Conclusions

The foregone conclusion fallacy is one of the most common errors in logic because we slip into it so easily and so unobtrusively. Suppose you've just discovered that the early symptoms of mercury poisoning are restlessness, instability, and irritability. Since ecologists have warned that our waters are polluted with mercury in dangerous amounts, and since everybody you know is restless, unstable, and irritable these days, you conclude that the population is succumbing to mercury poisoning. And we may well be, for that matter, but if you expect to convince anyone who wasn't already eager to make the same leap in logic, you'll need to garner more evidence—such as some medical reports showing that human beings (as well as fish and cattle) are actually ingesting dangerous amounts of the poison.

Dodging the Issue

There are a number of handy fallacies that people press into service in order to sidestep a problem while appearing to pursue the point. One of the most effective and the most underhanded—a favorite device of politicians—involves attacking the opponent, rather than the issue, and usually entails playing on emotional reactions, prejudices, fears, and ignorance instead of directly addressing the problem. You are probably familiar with the discrediting tactic which involves an appeal to popular opinion. If you would believe certain writers, the United Nations is trying to deliver the United States of America into the bloodstained hands of Soviet Russia; President Dwight D. Eisenhower was a willing tool of the Communist Party; the Supreme Court of the United States is dedicated to serving the interests of big business. A variation on the same approach goes like this:

> If we allow sex education to be taught in the public schools, the young will be corrupted, the moral fiber of the nation will be endangered, human beings will become no better than animals, and the Communists will just walk right in and take over.

Begging the Question

This common fallacy involves a circular argument: you offer as evidence premises which assume as true the very thing you're trying to prove. These premises, of course, are usually hidden or at least disguised; otherwise no one would even try this deception. Ex-Attorney General John Mitchell apparently considered his reasoning sound when he rejected the finding of the President's Commission on Obscenity that pornography is harmless:

> If we want a society of people who devote their time to base and sensuous things, then pornography may be harmless. But if we want a society in which the noble side of man is encouraged and mankind itself is elevated, then I submit that pornography is surely harmful.

Now, we could with hindsight observe that John Mitchell is hardly the person to instruct the citizenry about elevating the noble side of humanity. We could argue that it's better to have sensuous things than conspiracy, perjury, and obstruction of justice. But that would be *name-calling* or *ad hominem*—attacking the person rather than the issue. So let's look at his logic.

The basic issue that Mitchell is concerned with is the value of pornography. He appears to argue that pornography is undesirable by alluding to its baseness and by deploring its lack of elevating qualities. Yet by calling pornography base and ignoble, Mitchell is already *assuming* its undesirability. His argument is invalid since the truth of the conclusion is assumed in the premises. I happen to agree with Mitchell, by the way, that pornography can be harmful. But I still object to his statement on the grounds that he hasn't supplied any valid reasons.

Sliding Down the "Slippery Slope"

The *slippery-slope* fallacy assumes that one instance will automatically lead to thousands of similar instances, and thence directly to chaos. And that's not necessarily so. The *slippery-slope* argument goes like this: "If we grant this student's request to take the final examination early, then every student in the university will want to take early exams; so we'll have to deny the request."

KEEP AN OPEN MIND

All these techniques are frighteningly successful with untrained, unanalytical minds. And they get to many of us who are educated also. You should try never to use them, and you must be armed against them. Thinking is your best defense. *Think* while you're reading, and *think* some more before you write. Be prepared to change your mind. Instead of hunting for facts to shore up your present opinions, let the facts you gather lead you to a conclusion. And don't insist on a nice, tidy, clear-cut conclusion. There may not be one. Your conclusion may well be that both sides for various reasons have a point. Simply work to discover what you honestly believe to be the truth of the matter, and set that down as clearly and convincingly as you can.

Chapter 7

Writing About Your Reading: The Documented Essay

At some time you may be asked to write a paper that doesn't spring entirely from your own fertile brain. You may be expected to do research—to read fairly widely on a certain subject, to synthesize (to combine a number of different ideas into a new whole) and organize this accumulated information, and then get this new knowledge down on paper in clear and coherent prose.

Traditionally research papers involve *argument*. You may be expected to choose a topic which is somewhat controversial, investigate thoroughly the issues on both sides, and take a stand. Otherwise, the writing process for a research paper is the same as for any other. You'll still need to narrow the subject to a topic you can handle in the number of pages assigned. And you'll have to come up with a thesis statement and an outline before you begin writing. But first you'll locate the material you're going to read; then you'll take notes as you read so that you'll be able to give credit to various sources as you write the paper.

SCHEDULING YOUR RESEARCH PAPER

Writing a research paper is a time-consuming job. This is one paper that you simply cannot put off until the last minute. If you divide the project into units, you can keep the work under control.

Set Deadlines for Yourself

If your completed paper is due in, say, six weeks, you could put yourself on a schedule something like this:

1st week: Complete stack of cards listing possible sources. Try to narrow your topic down to a workable thesis question to investigate.

2d week: Read and take notes.
Settle on a preliminary thesis question.
Try to come up with a preliminary outline.

3d week: Continue reading and taking notes.

4th week: Complete reading and note taking.
Turn your thesis question into a statement.
Wrestle the outline into shape.

5th week: Write the first draft.
Let it cool—rest yourself.
Begin revising and editing.
Get someone reliable to read your second draft and tell you whether every sentence is clear, every quotation properly introduced, and every paragraph nicely coherent.

6th week: Polish the paper.
Type the final draft.
Let it rest at least overnight.
Proofread it carefully.

That is a fairly leisurely schedule. You can, of course, do the work in a shorter time if required to. You will just have to be more industrious about the reading. Some instructors deliberately ask students to complete the project within a month in order to allow no chance for procrastination. Whatever your time limit, devise a schedule for yourself and stick to it.

NARROWING YOUR TOPIC

If you have an area of interest but no ideas about any way to limit that topic, your first step might be to consult a good encyclopedia. Perhaps your father recently underwent abdominal surgery; as a result of spending many hours with him, you have become interested in hospitals. An encyclopedia article on hospitals will briefly discuss their history, some specialized kinds, services provided, intern training, difficulties with sanitation, and cost of care, among other things. Remembering that your dad contracted a staph infection while recovering from his operation, you might decide to investigate the problem of infections in hospitals. Why have they become prevalent? What is being done about them? Or, as you read the article, you might encounter a new term and become interested in *hospices*—specialized hospitals that attempt to provide comfort and dignity for the dying. Are these proving successful? Should we have more of them in this country? Something in an encyclopedia article on your subject is likely to provide the spark needed to fire your curiosity and give you a focus for your research.

EXPANDING YOUR ASSOCIATIONS

Once you have narrowed your topic, you may need momentarily to expand it again in order to locate all the relevant information in the library. As indexes and other reference tools do not necessarily classify information the way you do in your brain, you need to think of other headings under which your subject might be indexed. Before going to the library, you should make a list of topics related to your research subject. If you are planning to investigate hospices, your list might go like this:

Hospice	Geriatrics
Dying	Health care
Death	Old people
Aging	Euthanasia

Exercise   **7-1**

For each of the following subjects, list at least three related topics that
you could look under in reference books.

1 No-fault divorce
2 High school students' legal rights
3 Fad diets
4 Detective fiction by women
5 Use of the word *ain't*
6 Tax shelters
7 Horror movies

TOPICS FOR RESEARCHED WRITING

If your mind remains a blank and your instructor will allow you to
borrow a topic from this book, here are some ideas that might be interesting to research.

For Writing an Informative Paper

1 Research the history of a familiar product or object, such as Coca-
Cola, Mickey Mouse, the dictionary, the typewriter, the nectarine,
black mass, black magic, vampire movies.
2 Research and analyze a fad, craze, or custom: fraternity initiation,
pierced ears, "smile" buttons, any fad diet, punk fashions, Cabbage
Patch dolls.
3 How can autistic children be helped?
4 How can alcoholics be helped?
5 How can rape victims be helped?
6 Why do people become alcoholics?
7 What is *anorexia nervosa*, and can it be prevented?
8 What is *agoraphobia*, and what can be done about it?
9 How can battered women be helped?
10 Why do women allow themselves to be beaten by their husbands?

For Writing About Literature

1 How effective is the ending of *Huckleberry Finn*?

2 Is the governess sane or insane in James's "The Turn of the Screw"?

3 What are the characteristics of the "Hemingway hero"?

4 What are the mythological implications of Eudora Welty's "Moon Lake"?

5 What was Zola's contribution to literary naturalism?

For Persuasion or Argumentation

After doing the appropriate research, defend either side of one of the following issues:

1 Is nuclear waste disposal safe—or suicidal?

2 The use of animals in research should (should not) be allowed.

3 Clear-cutting of forests should (should not) be stopped.

4 It is (is not) better for children if their incompatible parents get a divorce.

5 The children's toys now on the market often encourage (discourage) destructiveness and discourage (encourage) creativity.

6 The federal government does (does not) have the right to monitor activities of U.S. citizens whom it regards as possible terrorists.

7 The fashion industry does (does not) exploit consumers. Or substitute any area of business that interests you: the cosmetics industry, the funeral business, the car manufacturers, the oil industry, etc.

8 Having a working mother does (does not) harm a child's development.

9 Automation has (has not) hindered our culture more than it has helped.

10 Violence on children's TV shows is (is not) harmful to children.

11 Newspaper reporters should (should not) have the right to protect their sources.

12 Parents should (should not) have the right to censor the textbooks and literature taught in their children's schools.

13 Internment of Japanese-American families after the United States entered World War II was a grave injustice (was necessary for the national security).

14 Is sexual harassment in the workplace a serious problem—or a myth?

15 The government should provide more (fewer) benefits for single parents on welfare.

SOME CLUES ON USING THE LIBRARY

Most college libraries offer orientation courses to show students how to find things in that clean, well-lighted place. If the course isn't required, take it anyway. An orientation course is your surest bet for learning your way around a library. If no such course is offered, your library will at least have available a handbook explaining what's where. A few minutes spent studying these instructions may save you many hours of aimless wandering. If after reading the handbook carefully you search and still can't find what you're looking for, ask for help. Librarians are seldom snarly about answering questions and will often take you in tow, lead you to the material you need, and give you valuable advice.

How to Find What You're Looking for If You Don't Know What It Is

When you begin making out a preliminary list of sources, you're looking for books, articles, and chapters in books on your topic, but you haven't the vaguest notion what these are or where to find them. Do not despair. What sounds like an impossible task is actually quite simple.

Begin with the Card or Computer Catalog

You will find the books available on your topic by looking it up by subject in the card catalog—or by using the handy computer, which provides the same information at the touch of a keyboard. Remember to look under related subjects if you fail to find enough material on your first try.

Remember also to have notecards handy when you begin this project, since you'll need to record authors, titles, and call numbers of any materials that appear useful. In the same area are the encyclopedias, the *Dictionary of National Biography* (British), and the *Dictionary of American Biography*, *Who's Who*, and various almanacs and dictionaries of famous quotations. These may or may not be of use to you, depending on what kind of research paper you're writing.

Indexes and Bibliographies   Things begin to get a bit tricky when you move onto the next step, which involves finding out what articles and essays are available on your topic. You'll find the chief tools you need in the reference room. These are mammoth sets of books which index, year by year, all the articles in a multitude of magazines.

You need to know first which indexes cover what type of magazines (or you could waste a lot of time scanning titles that have no potential usefulness). The *Readers' Guide to Periodical Literature* (familiarly known as the *Readers' Guide*) would be of little value if you're writing a paper on Edgar Allan Poe, for instance, because it indexes popular magazines, not scholarly ones. And how often does *Mechanics Illustrated* come out with a big spread on Poe? But if you're investigating the possibilities for cutting down pollution from automobile exhaust, *Mechanics Illustrated* may have just the article you want. Of if you're writing on some aspect of current events, the *Readers' Guide* will lead you to articles in *Newsweek*, *Time*, *U.S. News and World Report*, as well as to magazines which analyze current events, like *Harper's*, the *Atlantic*, and the *National Review*.

Another useful index for any research involving current events is the *Public Affairs Information Service Bulletin* (PAIS). Here you'll find indexed articles dealing with diverse topics of public interest. PAIS indexes the *Bulletin on Narcotics* published by the United Nations, the *Journal of Gerontology*, the *Journal of Forestry*, the *Journal of African and Asian Studies*, various legal journals, and countless other esoteric magazines and pamphlets.

For that Poe article, you'd be better off consulting the *Humanities Index* (formerly part of the *International Index*) or, if you want the really scholarly articles, the MLA *Bibliography* (which works just like the other indexes)—but you may have to troop off to the humanities area to find it. And if you'd like to find out what Poe's contemporaries thought of his writing, look him up in *Poole's Index to Periodical Literature*, which covers the major nineteenth-century magazines.

There are several other reference works of general interest. One of the most valuable is the *Essay and General Literature Index*. This treasure allows you to locate essays buried in books and to find chapters of books that may pertain to your topic, even though the title might give no clue. Then, there's the *Book Review Digest*, which tells you briefly what various reviewers thought of a book when it came out (if it came out since 1905) and gives you the information necessary to look up the actual review should you want to know more. All you need is the approximate year of publication in order to know which volume to consult. And the *New York Times Index* will furnish you with the date of any noteworthy event since 1851, allowing you to look it up in the files of your local newspaper—or in the *Times* itself, on microfilm. The *Social Sciences Index* (formerly part of the *International Index* and, until very recently, combined with the *Humanities Index*) should prove useful if you're looking for articles related to sociology, psychology, anthropology, political science, or economics. Articles pertaining to history or literature are listed in the *Humanities Index*.

One more tip: Just because some periodical index lists a magazine doesn't mean that your library will necessarily *have* that magazine. Before you tire yourself searching the stacks, spend a minute checking the list of periodical holdings for your library to find out whether the magazine will be there.

Also, just because a magazine or book is supposed to be in the library does not, in fact, guarantee that the item *will* be there. Theft is a major problem in libraries these days. You should report lost (or ripped off or ripped out) materials to someone at the circulation desk so that the missing materials can be noted and eventually replaced.

Ask About the Others   If you're planning some really high-powered research, you may need more specialized indexes than the ones discussed here. There are countless more covering every conceivable field. In order to use these, you'll need to go to the section of the library where the books and magazines in this field are located. Find a librarian in that area and ask for help.

SWEATING THROUGH THE RESEARCH

Once you've located the sources—the books and articles that you'll need to read and assimilate—you can begin the actual research.

Get It All Down

Every time you consult a new source, copy all the information necessary for indicating your source to the reader. If you fail to record all the pertinent data, you may find yourself tracking down a book or article weeks later in order to look up an essential publication date or volume

number that you neglected to record initially. The book may by this
time be checked out, lost, or stolen, so get it all down the first time.

You should probably use three- by five-inch notecards to keep
track of this information, and they should come out looking something
like the examples in Figures 7-1 through 7-4. Note the pertinent data.
Always get it *all*.

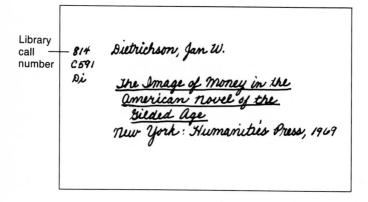

James E. Mulqueen
"Conservatism and Criticism:
The Literary Standards of
American Whigs, 1845–1852,"
American Literature, 41
Nov. 1969, 355–72.

Figure 7-1   Article from magazine with volume number.

Library
call
number

814
C591
Di

Dietrichson, Jan W.

The Image of Money in the
American Novel of the
Gilded Age
New York: Humanities Press, 1969

Figure 7-2   Book.

Library call number ────

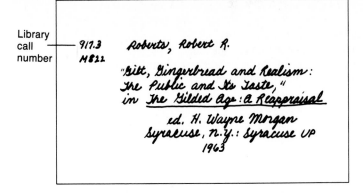

Figure 7-3 Essay in a collection.

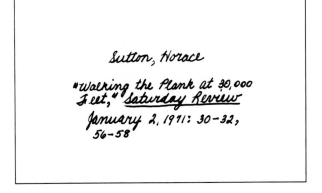

Figure 7-4 Article from magazine without volume number.

For Books:

1 Author or editor
2 Title (underlined)
3 Place of publication
4 Publisher
5 Date of publication (plus date of edition, if the book has more than one)
6 Call number at your library

For Articles:

1 Author (or "Anonymous")
2 Title (in quotation marks)
3 Name of magazine or newspaper (underlined)
4 Volume number (if the journal uses them)
5 Date of the issue
6 Pages the article covers

On to the Reading

Keeping your thesis in mind, you can get started on the reading. Have your notecards handy. At the same time you're doing your research, you'll be working out your outline. These notecards, each containing information related to a single idea, can be shuffled around later and slipped into appropriate sections of your outline. Taking notes consecutively on regular sheets of paper makes this handy sorting of ideas impossible.

As you take notes, put subject headings in the upper righthand corner of your notecards indicating in a word or two what each note is about. Eventually these subject headings will probably correspond to sections of your outline. Chances are that your outline won't really take shape until you're fairly well along with your research—possibly not until you've finished it. As you collect more and more cards, leaf through them occasionally to see if they can be arranged into three or four main categories to form the major headings of an outline. The sooner you can get one worked out, the more efficient becomes your research. You can see exactly what you're looking for and avoid taking notes that would eventually prove off the point and have to be discarded.

But if an idea sounds potentially useful, copy it down whether it fits exactly or not. If the idea recurs in your reading and gathers significance, you may decide to add a section to your outline or to expand one of the present sections. Then later, at the organizing stage, if you have cards with ideas that just don't seem to fit in anywhere, let them go. Let them go cheerfully. Don't ruin the focus and unity of your paper by trying to wedge in every single note you've taken. Unless you're an uncommonly cautious notetaker, you'll have a number of cards that you can't use.

Your notecards may look something like the one shown in Figure 7-5.

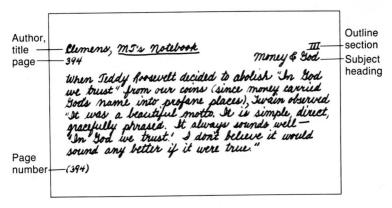

Author, title page

Outline section
Subject heading

Page number

Clemens, MT's notebook   III
394   *money & God*

When Teddy Roosevelt decided to abolish "In God we trust" from our coins (since money carried God's name into profane places), Twain observed "It was a beautiful motto. It is simple, direct, gracefully phrased. It always sounds well— 'In God we trust.' I don't believe it would sound any better if it were true."

(394)

Figure 7-5 Sample notecard.

Again, don't forget to record *on each card*:

1 Author's last name
2 Abbreviated title
3 Page number

If you'll get in the habit of writing down these essentials before you take the note, there's less chance of forgetting an item—or all the items, for that matter.

TIPS ON AVOIDING PLAGIARISM

Plagiarism, as you know, means using somebody else's writing without giving proper credit. You can avoid this dishonesty by using a moderate amount of care in taking notes. Put quotation marks around any material—however brief—that you copy verbatim. As you're leafing through the cards trying to sort them into categories, circle these quotation marks with a red pencil so you can't miss them. There remains the problem of avoiding the author's phrasing if you decide not to quote directly but to paraphrase. This dilemma is not so easily solved.

You naturally tend to write the idea down using the same phrasing, changing or omitting a few words. This close paraphrasing is, in the minds of many, still plagiarism. To escape it, you must not even look at your source as you take notes that aren't direct quotations. I suggest that you use both methods—verbatim notes and summarizing notes— and let the summaries be just that, condensing several pages of reading on a single card. You'll scarcely be able to fall into the author's phrasing that way. Or if your writer uses an eyecatching phrase— something like Veblen's "code of pecuniary honor"—get that down in quotation marks in the middle of your summary. A summarizing notecard will look something like the card shown in Figure 7-6.

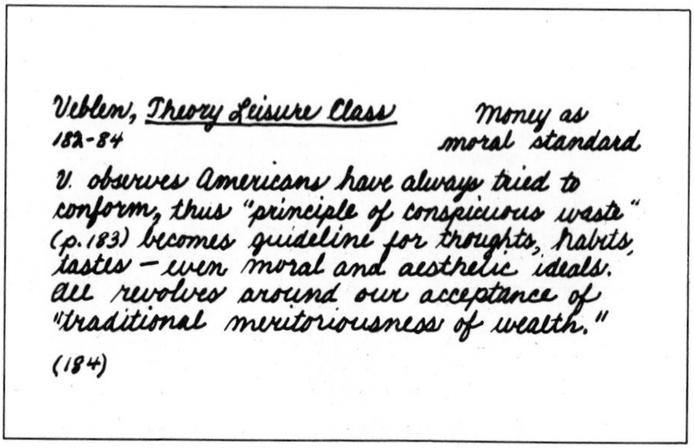

Figure 7-6 Summary notecard.

Paraphrase Carefully

Sometimes, of course, you must do fairly close paraphrasing of important ideas. Since plagiarism is often accidental, let me give you a couple of examples to show you exactly what plagiarism is. Here is a passage from Marvin Harris's *Cows, Pigs, Wars, and Witches: The Riddles of Culture* (1978), which, let's assume, you need to use in making a point in your paper:

> No one understood better than Gandhi that cow love had different implications for rich and poor. For him the cow was the central focus of the struggle to rouse India to authentic nationhood.

If you incorporate that material into your paper in the following words, you have plagiarized, even though you've cited Harris as your source:

> Gandhi understood the different implications of cow love for rich and poor. He saw the struggle to rouse India to authentic nationhood focused on the cow (Harris 21).

The fact that the source is cited suggests that this plagiarism might have resulted from ignorance rather than deception, but it is plagiarism nonetheless. Changing a few words or rearranging the phrases is not enough. Here is another version, somewhat less blatant but still plagiarism:

> Gandhi well knew that rich and poor were affected differently by cow love, which he saw as a means of inspiring his people to authentic nationhood (Harris 21).

There are still two phrases there that are distinctly Harris's: *cow love* and *authentic nationhood*. It is quite all right to use those phrases but *only if you put them in quotation marks.* You should also acknowledge your source in the text of your paper—as well as in your citation— whenever possible, like this:

> According to Harris, Gandhi well knew that rich and poor were affected differently by "cow love," which he saw as a means of inspiring his people "to authentic nationhood" (21).

Notice, by the way, that the phrase *rich and poor* in the original does not appear in quotation marks in this acceptable version. The phrase is so simple, so commonly used—and so nearly impossible to replace without using many more words—that quotation marks are unnecessary. Here is another acceptable version in which none of the original phrasing is used:

> Harris suggests that Gandhi well knew that rich and poor were affected differently by reverence for the sacred cow but saw this symbol as a means of uniting his people (21).

REMEMBER: **If you are paraphrasing, put the passage into your own words; if you are quoting directly, put the passage in quotation marks.**

FINISHING THE PAPER

After you've read all the material you feel is necessary to cover your topic thoroughly, gather up your notecards and shuffle them to fit the sections of your outline. If your outline is still hanging fire, now is the time to wrestle it into shape. The actual writing of the paper is the same as writing any other paper, except that you'll incorporate the material from the notecards into your text (either in your own words or through direct quotes) and give credit to the original authors for ideas borrowed and actual passages quoted. The following sections will give you advice on how to handle quotations and documentation (crediting the quotations).

To Quote or Not to Quote

Never quote directly unless (1) the material is authoritative and convincing evidence in support of your thesis, or (2) the statement is happily phrased, or (3) the idea is controversial and you need to assure your readers that you aren't slanting or misinterpreting the source. You would want, for instance, to quote directly an observation as well-put as this one:

> Bernard Rosenberg defines "pragmatism" as "a distinctly American philosophy whose only failing is that it does not work."

There is no need, however, for the direct quotation in the following sentence:

> The ICC, in an effort to aid the rail industry, has asked for a "federal study of the need and means for preserving a national passenger service."

You could phrase that just as well yourself. But remember, even after you put the statement into your own words, you'll still need to indicate where you got the information.

Quoting Quotations

Sometimes in your reading you will come across a quotation that says exactly what you have been hoping to find. If the quotation is complete enough to serve your purpose, and if you honestly don't think you would benefit from tracking down the original, then don't bother. Instead, include that quotation in the usual way. But notice that your citation will include "qtd. in" before the source and page number:

> George Cukor once told Scott Fitzgerald, "I've only known two people who eat faster than you and I, and they are both dead now" (qtd. in Latham 39).

> Mark Twain relates that he once knew a Miss Sexton, who pronounced her name "Saxton to make it finer, the nice, kindhearted, smirky, smily dear Christian creature" (qtd. in Wecter 103).

Working Quotations in Smoothly

If you want your research paper to read smoothly, you must take care in incorporating quotations into your own writing. You must have ready a supply of introductory phrases with which to slide them in gracefully—phrases like "As Quagmire discovered," "Professor Clyde Crashcup notes," and "According to Dr. Dimwit." If you run through the examples in this section on quoting, you will find a generous assortment of these phrases. Borrow them with my blessing.

Notice, please, that the more famous the person, the less likely we are to use Mr., Miss, Mrs., or Ms. in front of the name. "Mr. Milton" sounds quite droll. If the person has a title, you can use it or not, as you think appropriate: Dr. Pasteur or Pasteur, Sir Winston Churchill or Churchill, President Lincoln or Lincoln.

Introduce Your Quotations   Most of the time you will introduce a quotation before beginning it, like this:

> As Mark Twain observed, "Heaven for climate, hell for society."*

But you may want to break one up in the middle every so often for variety, this way:

---

*I have omitted many citations in this book to save space. But remember, you do not have this option in a documented paper. Whenever you quote directly, you *must* cite the source.

"But if thought corrupts language," cautions George Orwell, "language can also corrupt thought."

Or you can make most of the sentence yours and quote only the telling phrases or key ideas of your authority, like this:

Lily B. Campbell considers King Henry's inability to fight "a saintly weakness."

Or this:

The play's effectiveness lies, as E. M. W. Tillyard points out, in "the utter artlessness of the language."

But do introduce your quotations, please. The MLA (Modern Language Association) documentation style suggests identifying the source within the citation immediately following the quotation. But I think that identifying the source before presenting the borrowed material allows your readers a clearer understanding of which ideas are yours and which come from sources.

If you have difficulty introducing your authorities gracefully in the text of your paper, perhaps you are using too many direct quotations.

Make the Grammar Match   When you integrate a quotation into your own sentence, you are responsible for making sure that the entire sentence makes sense. You must adjust the way your sentence is worded so that the grammar comes out right. Read your quotations over carefully to be sure they don't end up like this one:

When children are born, their first reactions are "those stimuli which constitute their environment."

"Reactions" are not "stimuli." The sentence should read this way:

When children are born, their first reactions are to "those stimuli which constitute their environment."

What a difference a word makes—the difference here between sense and nonsense. Take particular care when you are adding someone else's words to your own; you get the blame if the words in the quotation do not make sense, because they *did* make sense before you lifted them out of context.

Use Special Punctuation   When you write a documented paper, you probably will need to use some rather specialized marks of punctuation: *ellipsis dots* (to show that you have omitted something from a quotation) and *brackets* (to make an editorial comment within a quotation). You will find both of these useful devices discussed fully in the alphabetized ''Revising Index,'' Chapter 8.

To Cite or Not to Cite

The main purpose of documentation—of citing sources used in a research paper—is to give credit for ideas, information, and actual phrasing that you borrow from other writers. You cite sources in order to be honest and to lend authority to your own writing. You also include citations to enable your readers to find more extensive information than your paper furnishes, in case they become engrossed in your subject and want to read some of your sources in full.

We are all troubled occasionally about when a citation is necessary. I can say with authority that you must include a citation for:

1 All direct quotations
2 All indirect quotations
3 All major ideas that are not your own
4 All essential facts, information, and statistics that are not general knowledge—especially anything controversial

The last category is the one that causes confusion. In general, the sort of information available in an encyclopedia does not need a citation. But statements interpreting, analyzing, or speculating on such information should be documented. If you say that President Warren G. Harding died in office, you do not need a citation because that is a widely known and undisputed fact. If you say that Harding's administration was one of the most corrupt in our history, most people would not feel the need for a citation because authorities agree that the Harding scandals were flagrant and enormous. But if you say that Harding was sexually intimate with a young woman in the White House cloakroom while President of the United States, I strongly suggest that you cite your source. Because such information is not widely known and is also debatable, you need to identify your source so that your readers can judge the reliability of your evidence. Then, too, they might want further enlightenment on the matter, and your citation will lead them to a more complete discussion. Probably it's better to bother your readers with too many citations than to have them question your integrity by having too few.

Accuracy Is the Aim

After years of being told to be original, to be creative, to think for yourself, you are now going to be told—on this one matter, at least—to fall into line and slavishly follow the authorities. What you might consider a blessed bit of variety will not be appreciated in the slightest. If you put a period after the first citation, put a period after every one. Get the form correct every time, right down to the last comma, colon, and parenthesis.

The information (date, publisher, place of publication) necessary for completing a citation is located on the title page and on the back of the title page of each book. For magazines you usually can find it all on the cover.

When in Doubt, Use Common Sense

Keep in mind that the purpose of documentation is dual:

1 To give credit to your sources
2 To allow your readers to find your sources in case they want further information on the subject

If you are ever in doubt about documentation form (if you are citing something so unusual that you cannot find a similar entry in the samples here), use your common sense and give credit the way you think it logically should be done. Be as consistent as possible with other citations.

REVISING THE PAPER

Since a research paper requires the incorporation of other people's ideas and the acknowledgment of these sources, you need to take special care in revising.

Check the Usual Things

1 Be sure the introduction states your thesis.
2 Be sure each paragraph is unified, coherent, and directly related to your thesis.
3 Be sure the transitions between paragraphs are smooth.
4 Be sure your conclusion evaluates the results of your research; if the paper is argumentative, be sure the last sentence is emphatic.

Check the Special Things

1 Be sure that you have introduced direct quotations gracefully, using the name and, if possible, the occupation of the person quoted.
2 Be sure each citation is accurate.
3 Be sure that paraphrases are in your own words and that the sources are clearly acknowledged.
4 Be sure to underline the titles of books and magazines; put quotation marks around the titles of articles and chapters in books.
5 Be sure that you have written most of the paper yourself; you need to examine, analyze, or explain the material, not just splice together a bunch of quotations and paraphrases.
6 Be sure always to separate quotations with some comment of your own.
7 Be sure to use ellipsis dots if you omit any words from a quotation that your readers would not otherwise know were missing; never leave out anything that alters the meaning of a sentence.
8 Be sure to use square brackets, not parentheses, if you add words or change verb tenses in a quotation.
9 Be sure that you have not relied too heavily on a single source.
10 Be sure to indent long quotations ten spaces—without quotation marks.

Before you work on your final draft, give your entire attention to the following instructions on form.

Preparing the Final Draft

1 Provide margins of at least one inch at the top, bottom, and sides.

2 Double-space throughout.

3 Do not put the title of your paper in quotation marks.

4 Insert corrections neatly in ink *above the line* (if allowed by your instructor).

5 Put page numbers in the upper-right-hand corner. But do not number the title page or the first page of the paper. After the title page and the outline, count all pages in the total as you number. Note correct page numbering on the sample student paper, which follows.

6 Proofread. You may well be close to exhaustion by the time you finish copying your paper, and the last thing you will feel like doing is rereading the blasted thing. But force yourself. Or force somebody else. But do not skip the proofreading. It would be a shame to allow careless errors to mar an otherwise excellent paper.

SAMPLE STUDENT RESEARCH PAPER

The following documented essay was written by Kathy M. Donaldson, a student at Illinois State University. Kathy chose to follow the new MLA (Modern Language Association) style commonly used in the humanities. Complete instruction for employing this documentation style follows Kathy's paper.

If you once learned the old MLA style and would feel more comfortable using it, you will find instruction for its use on pages 155–161.

Cover Page

Getting Down to Business with the Liberal Arts

Kathy M. Donaldson

English 145

Professor Susan Day

Getting Down to Business with the Liberal Arts

Prospective graduates in liberal arts fields listen to an accusation that is akin to the sound of nails on a chalkboard from the time they enter the field to the time they receive the sheepskin: "You'll never get a decent job with a liberal arts degree." This liberal arts major is tired of the misbegotten preconceptions of many individuals who view the liberal arts as a luxury that has no value outside the classroom. The business world is currently reporting that a specialized business degree is often not the answer to their administrative employment needs. A number of surveys and articles, produced for and by businesses, report that an overwhelming quantity of technically trained people do not possess the skills needed to guide them to careers in middle and upper management. Experience is still the best teacher, and experience is shining the spotlight on the liberal arts graduates who "are getting offers that rival the stuff of M.B.A.s' dreams" (Byrne 112).

According to William Benton, the outpouring of technically trained graduates is a direct result "of the age of the pat answer" (v). Many students are not choosing their majors on the basis of their interests or their natural abilities. Instead, says Lynne Cheney, business writer for Newsweek, ". . . they are channeling themselves into fields that promise to be profitable: business, engineering, computer science, allied health programs" (7). These fields of study do provide pat answers for their students. However, most of life is not easily reduced to textbook answers, and therein lies the problem. When the answer is not available, the specialized graduates are often trapped because they have not been taught the skills necessary to creatively formulate a solution.

Despite this fact, the trend today is for students to flock to the specialized fields that are currently offering the greatest salary potential. What happens to the specialized graduates when their chosen fields are no longer "hot" and the jobs dwindle? It is difficult, at best, to predict which skills will be demanded years down the road. Therefore, Cheney counsels that ". . . a student's best career preparation is one that emphasizes general understanding and intellectual curiosity: a knowledge of how to learn and the desire to do it. Literature, history, philosophy and the social sciences . . . are the ones traditionally believed to develop such habits of mind" (7).

The surfacing realization that the liberal arts

offer the kind of quality education favorable to

business is being reiterated by several top executives

who are now voicing their preferences. Arthur F.

Oppenheimer, president of Oppenheimer Companies,

Inc., asserts that today's management needs the

skills of creative and independent thinking, the

ability "to make decisions when all the data required

to solve the problem are not available; . . . not to rely

on quantitative and analytical data, . . . to avoid the

obvious and solely subjective. . . . These are all abili-

ties fostered by the liberal arts" (qtd. in Sturman 57–

58). In agreement with Mr. Oppenheimer is the

president of Chemical Bank, Robert Callander, who

claims that ". . . a liberally educated person is still

the type of individual needed at the highest levels of

corporate life. . . . The technical skills are built upon

this base'' (qtd. in Bennett 62–63). General Motors

chair, Roger E. Smith, is also in concurrence when

he explains in Management Review the valuable role

creativity plays in the corporate world. Creativity,

he claims, is necessary

> to see relations between things that may
> seem utterly different, and . . . to connect
> the seemingly unconnected. The power is
> quite familiar to people trained to recog-
> nize the recurring elements and the
> common themes in art, literature and
> history. (36)

Certainly, the importance of creativity in

business should not be ignored. However, the top

contender among skills necessary to succeed in

business is indisputable—effective communication.

In a nationwide survey, chief executives ranked

verbal communication skills at the top of the list for

success in middle and top business positions; these

same executives ranked writing skills first by a large

margin in a list of deficiencies reported by business

(Warren 12). A working knowledge of communica-

tion skills is quite often lacking in the specialized

graduate.

> But students of drama, language, litera-
> ture, speech and rhetoric do understand
> what [good communication entails]. They
> learn to arrange their thoughts in logical
> order, and to write and speak clearly,
> economically, and unpretentiously.
> They learn to communicate with a real
> feeling for the flexibility and power of
> language, and with a sensitivity to their
> own purposes and to the needs of their
> audience. (Smith 38)

These corporate leaders exhibit a growing

preference for liberal arts graduates that is filtering

down from the executives to those responsible for

hiring quality people. First Boston Bank, for

example, recently hired graduates for 42 financial

analyst positions. The final tally disclosed that 90
percent were liberal arts graduates (Byrne 114).
Liberal arts graduates experience upward mobility
after the initial hiring, too. Thirty-eight percent of
today's chief executive officers are liberal arts graduates, and the New York Times disclosed that nine of
IBM's top thirteen executives are liberal arts majors
(Cheney 7).

AT&T has also released some interesting facts
about their graduates of the liberal arts in a recently
completed study. Their data reveals that:

—Liberal arts graduates enjoyed more mobility
than any other group.
—More than twice as many liberal arts graduates made it to senior management than did
those with engineering degrees.

—Liberal arts graduates beat business degree
holders in having the best overall records for
managerial performance and progress (Byrne
114).

Success stories of liberal arts graduates are
often unknown by the general public. Following are
the names of well-known figures shown with
positions they currently hold or have held in the
past. All were educated in liberal arts fields (Cheney
7):

Name	Position	Degree
Thomas Wayman	Chair, Columbia Broadcasting System	English
Cathleen Black	Publisher, USA Today	English
William Raspberry	Columnist, Washington Post	History

Name	Position	Degree
Tom Brokaw	Anchorman, NBC	Political Science
George Schultz	Secretary of State	Economics
John Herrington	Secretary of Energy	Economics
Donald Hodel	Interior Secretary	Government
Elizabeth Dole	Transportation Secretary	Political Science
James Baker	Secretary of Treasury	History
Ronald Reagan	President	Economics and Sociology
William Bennett	Secretary of Education	Philosophy
Pat Buchanan	Communications Director	English and Philosophy
Donald Regan	Chief of Staff (former head of Merrill Lynch)	English
Malcolm Baldrige	Secretary of Commerce	English

The list could go on and serves to demonstrate that students with a degree in liberal arts are not crippled by their chosen course of study. A liberal arts degree can unlock doors in virtually any facet of life. The Chief Executive Officer of Time, Inc., Dick Munro, states his employment preference with no qualms: "I would personally opt for a liberal arts graduate every time. Almost all the CEOs I know are liberal arts graduates. We still think that liberal arts institutions are putting out the best product" (qtd. in Sturman 58). Thanks to Mr. Munro and other progressive business leaders, liberal arts graduates are indeed being given the opportunity to exercise their diverse skills in the business world and are proving wrong those who said they would never make it.

Works Cited

Bennett, William J. "The Humanities Pay Off."

Across the Board Apr. 1985: 61–63.

Benton, William. Introduction. Great Ideas from the

Great Books. By Mortimer J. Adler. New

York: Washington Square P, 1961. v.

Byrne, John A. "Let's Hear It for Liberal Arts."

Forbes 1 Jly. 1985: 112+.

Cheney, Lynne V. "Students of Success." Newsweek

1 Sept. 1986: 7.

Smith, Roger B. "Humanities & Business: The Twain

Shall Meet—But How?" Management Review

Apr. 1985: 36–39.

Sturman, Emanuel. "Do Corporations Really Want

Liberal Arts Grads?'' Management Review Sept.

1986: 657–59.

Warren, Russell G. New Links Between General

Education and Business Careers. Washington,

DC: Association of American Colleges, 1983. 12.

THE MLA DOCUMENTATION STYLE

The simplified new MLA documentation style resembles those used in other academic disciplines. It works like this:

A   Mention your source (author's last name and page number) within the text of your paper in parentheses, like this:

> One of the great all-time best-sellers, <u>Uncle Tom's Cabin</u>,
>
> sold over 300,000 copies in America and more than 2
>
> million copies worldwide (Wilson 3).

B   Your readers can identify this source by consulting your "Works Cited" list at the end of your paper (see items I through N). The entry for the information above would appear like this:

> Wilson, Edmund. <u>Patriotic Gore: Studies in the Literature</u>
>
> <u>of the American Civil War</u>. New York: Oxford UP,
>
> 1966.

C   If you are quoting directly or if you want to stress the authority of the source you are paraphrasing, you may mention the name of the source in your sentence. Then include just the page number (or numbers) at the end in parentheses, like this:

> In <u>Patriotic Gore</u>, Edmund Wilson tells us that Mrs. Stowe
>
> felt "the book had been written by God" (5).

D   If you must quote indirectly—something quoted from another source not available to you—indicate this in your parenthetical reference by using "qtd. in" (for "quoted in"). The following example comes from a book written by Donald Johanson and Maitland Edey:

> Richard Leakey's wife, Maeve, told the paleoanthropologist

David Johanson, ''We heard all about your bones on the

radio last night'' (qtd. in Johanson and Edey 162).

E   If you are using a source written or edited by more than three
people, use only the name of the first person listed, followed by ''et
al.'' (meaning ''and others''):

Blair et al. observe that the fine arts were almost ignored

by colonial writers (21).

F   If you refer to more than one work by the same author, include a
shortened title in the citation in your text:

(Huxley, <u>Brave</u> 138).

G   If the author's name is not given, then use a shortened title instead.
In your abbreviation, be sure to use at least the first word of the full
title to send the reader to the proper alphabetized entry on your ''Works
Cited'' page. The following is a reference to a newspaper article
entitled ''Ramifications of Baboon Use Expected to Become an Issue'':

The doctor observed that some people objected to the trans-

plant on grounds that were emotional rather than rational

(''Ramifications'' A23).

H   If you are quoting more than *four* typed lines, you should indent
the quotation ten spaces and omit the quotation marks. Cite the page
number in parentheses two spaces after the period:

About Nora in Ibsen's <u>A Doll's House</u>, Liv Ullman writes,

She says goodbye to everything that is familiar

and secure. She does not walk through the door

to find somebody else to live with and for; she is

leaving the house more insecure than she ever

realized she could be. But she hopes to find out

who she is and why she is.   (263)

I   On your last page, a separate page, alphabetize your "Works Cited" list of all sources mentioned in your paper. Use *hanging indention*: that is, after the first line of each entry, indent the other lines five spaces.

J   In your "Works Cited" list, in citing two or more works by the same author, give the name in the first entry only. Thereafter, in place of the name, type three hyphens and a period, skip two spaces, then follow with the usual information. Alphabetize the entries by title:

Lewis, C. S. The Dark Tower and Other Stories. Ed. Walter

Hooper. New York: Harcourt, 1977.

———. The Screwtape Letters. New York: Macmillan,

1976.

K   Omit any mention of *page* or *pages* or *line* or *lines*: do not even include abbreviations for these terms. Use numbers alone.

L   Abbreviate publishers' names. See the list of abbreviations suggested by the MLA on pages 147 through 149.

M   Use regular (not roman) numerals throughout. Exception: James I, Elizabeth II. Use *lowercase* roman numerals for citing page numbers from a preface, introduction, or table of contents. You may use roman numerals to indicate act and scene in plays: "In *Hamlet* III.ii, the action shifts. . . ."

N   Use raised note numbers for *informational notes* only (i.e., notes containing material pertinent to your discussion but not precisely to the point). Include these content notes at the end of your paper on a separate page just before your "Works Cited" list, and entitle them "Notes."

O   If you are writing about literature, you should cite the edition of the novel, play, short story, or poetry collection you are using in an informational note. Thereafter, include the page numbers in parentheses in the text of the paper. The note should read like this:

[1]Joyce Carol Oates, "Accomplished Desires," in

Wheel of Love and Other Stories. Greenwich: Fawcett,

1970: 127. All further references to this work appear in

parentheses in the text.

Your subsequent acknowledgments in the text will be done this way:

Dorie was not consoled, although Mark "slid his big beefy

arms around her and breathed his liquory love into her

face, calling her his darling, his beauty" (129).

Note the placement of the quotation marks—before the parentheses, which are followed by the period. *But* if the quotation is a long one that you need to indent without quotation marks, the period comes *before* the parentheses as shown in item H above.

Sample Entries for a "Works Cited" List

The following models will help you write "Works Cited" entries for most of but not all the sources you will use. If you use a source not treated in these samples, consult the more extensive list of sample entries found in the new *MLA Handbook* or ask your instructor.

Books

Book by one author:

Abernathy, Charles F. Civil Rights: Cases and

Materials. St. Paul: West, 1980.

’ or more books by the same author:

’, Stephen Jay. The Mismeasure of Man. New York:

Norton, 1981.

———. The Panda's Thumb: More Reflections in Natural

   History. New York: Norton, 1980.

3 Book by two or three authors:

   Brusaw, Charles, Gerald J. Alfred, and Walter E. Oliu. The

      Business Writer's Handbook. New York: St.

      Martin's, 1976.

   Ciardi, John, and M. Williams. How Does a Poem Mean?

      Rev. ed. Boston: Houghton, 1975.

4 Book by more than three authors:

   Sheridan, Marion C., et al. The Motion Picture and the

      Teaching of English. New York: Appleton, 1965.

[The phrase "et al." is an abbreviation for "et alii," meaning "and others."]

5 Book by an anonymous author:

   Beowulf. Trans. Kevin Crossley-Holland. New York:

      Farrar, 1968.

6 Book with an editor:

   Zaranka, William, ed. The Brand-X Anthology of Poetry.

      Cambridge: Apple-Wood, 1981.

[For a book with two or more editors, use "eds."]

7 Book with an editor and an author:

   Shakespeare, William. Shakespeare: Major Plays and th

Sonnets. Ed. G. B. Harrison. New York: Harcourt,

1948.

8 Work in a collection or anthology:

Firebaugh, Joseph J. "The Pragmatism of Henry James."

Henry James's Major Novels: Essays in Criticism.

Ed. Lyall Powers. East Lansing: Michigan State P,

1973. 187-201.

Pirandello, Luigi. Six Characters in Search of an Author.

The Norton Anthology of World Masterpieces. Ed.

Maynard Mack et al. 5 ed. 2 vols. New York:

Norton, 1985. 2:1387-1432.

9 Work reprinted in a collection or anthology:

Sage, George H. "Sport in American Society: Its Pervasive-

ness and Its Study." Sport and American

Society. 3rd ed. Reading: Addison-Wesley, 1980.

4-15. Rpt. in Physical Activity and the Social

Sciences. Ed. W. Neil Widmeyer. 5th ed. Ithaca:

Movement, 1983. 42-52.

[First give complete data for the earlier publication; then give the reprinted source.]

10 Multivolume work:

Blom, Eric, ed. Grove's Dictionary of Music and Musicians.

5th ed. 10 vols. New York: St. Martin's, 1961.

11 Reprinted (republished) book:

> Malamud, Bernard. <u>The Natural</u>. 1952. New York: Avon,
>
> 1980.

12 Later edition:

> Gibaldi, Joseph, and Walter S. Achtert. <u>MLA Handbook for</u>
>
> <u>Writers of Research Papers</u>. 2nd ed. New York:
>
> MLA, 1984.

13 Book in translation:

> de Beauvoir, Simone. <u>The Second Sex</u>. Trans. H. M.
>
> Parshley. New York: Knopf, 1971.

[Alphabetize this entry under *B*.]

Newspapers

14 Signed newspaper article:

> Krebs, Emilie. "Sewer Backups Called No Problem."
>
> <u>Pantagraph</u> [Bloomington, IL] 20 Nov. 1985: A3.

[If the city of publication is not apparent from the name of the
newspaper give the city and state in brackets after the newspaper's
name as shown above.]

> Weiner, Jon. "Vendetta: The Government's Secret War
>
> Against John Lennon." <u>Chicago Tribune</u> 5 Aug.
>
> 1984, Sec. 3:1.

[Note the difference between ''A3'' in the first example and ''sec. 3:1'' in the second. Both refer to section and page, but in the first the pagination appears as ''A3'' in the newspaper, whereas in the second the section designation is not part of the pagination.]

15 Unsigned newspaper article:

> ''Minister Found Guilty of Soliciting Murder.'' New York
>
> Times 2 Aug. 1984: A12.

16 Letter to the editor:

> Kessler, Ralph. ''Orwell Defended.'' Letter. New York
>
> Times Book Review 15 Dec. 1985: 26.

17 Editorial:

> ''From Good News to Bad.'' Editorial. Washington
>
> Post 16 July 1984: 10.

Magazines and Journals

18 Article from a monthly or bimonthly magazine:

> Foulkes, David. ''Dreams of Innocence.'' Psychology
>
> Today Dec. 1978: 78-88.

> Lawren, Bill. ''1990's Designer Beasts.'' Omni Nov. 1985:
>
> 56-61.

19 Article from a weekly or biweekly magazine (signed and unsigned):

> Adler, Jerry. ''A Voyager's Close-Up of
>
> Saturn.'' Newsweek 7 Sept. 1981: 57-58.

> ''Warning: 'Love' for Sale.'' Newsweek Nov. 1985: 39.

20   Article from a magazine with continuous pagination: *(Continuous numbering of pages)*

> Potvin, Raymond, and Che-Fu Lee. "Multistage Path
>
>> Models of Adolescent Alcohol and Drug Use."
>>
>> Journal of Studies on Alcohol 41 (1980): 531-542.

21   Article from a magazine that paginates each issue separately or that uses only issue numbers:

> Terkel, Studs. "The Good War: An Oral History of World War
>
>> II." Atlantic 254.1 (July 1984): 45-75.

[That is, volume 254, issue 1.]

Other Sources

22   Review (of a book):

> Langer, Elinor. "Life Under Apartheid: The Possible and
>
>> the Real." Rev. of A Revolutionary Woman, by Sheila
>>
>> Fugard. Ms. Nov. 1985: 26-27.

23   Personal or telephone interview:

> Deau, Jeanne. Personal interview. 12 Mar. 1983.

> Vidal, Gore. Telephone interview. 2 June 1984.

[Treat published interviews like articles, with the person being interviewed as the author.]

24   Published letter:

> Tolkien, J. R. R. "To Sam Gamgee." 18 Mar. 1956. Letter
>
>> 184 in The Letters of J. R. R. Tolkien. Ed.
>>
>> Humphrey Carpenter. Boston: Houghton,
>>
>> 1981. 244-245.

25 Unpublished letter:

Wharton, Edith. Letter to William Brownell. 6 Nov. 1907.

Wharton Archives. Amherst College, Amherst.

Isherwood, Christopher. Letter to the author. 24 Apr.

1983.

26 Anonymous pamphlet:

How to Help a Friend with a Drinking Problem. American

College Health Association, 1984.

Aaron Copland: A Catalogue of His Works. New York:

Boosey, n.d.

[The abbreviation "n.d." means "no date given."]
27 Article from a specialized dictionary:

Van Doren, Carl. "Samuel Langhorne Clemens." DAB.

1958 ed.

[Some commonly used resources, such as the *Dictionary of American Biography*, have accepted abbreviations.]
28 Encyclopedia article (signed and unsigned):

Martin, William R. "Drug Abuse." World Book Encyclo-

pedia. 1983 ed.

"Scapegoat." Encyclopaedia Britannica: Micropaedia.

1979 ed.

[The micropaedia is volumes 1–10 of the *Britannica*.]

29 Bible:

> The Holy Bible. Revised Standard Version. Cleveland:
>
>> World, 1962.
>
> The Jerusalem Bible. Trans. Alexander Jones et al.
>
>> Garden City: Doubleday, 1966.

[Do not list the Bible unless you use a version other than the King James. Cite chapter and verse in parentheses in the text of your paper this way: (Rom. 12.4–8). Underline only the titles of Bibles other than the King James version.]

30 Film:

> Wyler, William, dir. Wuthering Heights. With Merle
>
>> Oberon and Laurence Olivier. Samuel Goldwyn,
>
>> 1939.

[If you are citing the work of an actor or screenwriter, put that person's name first.]

31 Lecture:

> Albee, Edward. 'A Dream or a Nightmare?" Illinois State
>
>> University Fine Arts Lecture. Normal, 18 Mar. 1979.

Note: For any other sources (such as television shows, recordings, works of art), you should remember to include enough information to permit an interested reader to locate your original source. Be sure to arrange this information in a logical fashion, duplicating so far as possible the order and punctuation of the entries above. To be on safe ground, consult your instructor for suggestions about documenting unusual material.

Standard Abbreviations of Publishers' Names

Allyn	Allyn and Bacon, Inc.
Appleton	Appleton-Century-Crofts
Ballantine	Ballantine Books, Inc.
Bantam	Bantam Books, Inc.
Basic	Basic Books
Bobbs	Bobbs-Merrill Co., Inc.
Bowker	R. R. Bowker Co.
Cambridge UP	Cambridge University Press
Clarendon	Clarendon Press
Columbia UP	Columbia University Press
Cornell UP	Cornell University Press
Crown	Crown Publishers, Inc.
Dell	Dell Publishing Co., Inc.
Dial	Dial Press, Inc.
Dodd	Dodd, Mead, and Co.
Doubleday	Doubleday and Co., Inc.
Dover	Dover Publications, Inc.
Dutton	E. P. Dutton
Farrar	Farrar, Straus, and Giroux, Inc.
Feminist	Feminist Press
Free	Free Press
GPO	Government Printing Office
Grove	Grove Press, Inc.
Harcourt	Harcourt Brace Jovanovich, Inc.
Harper	Harper & Row Publishers, Inc.
Harvard UP	Harvard University Press
Heath	D. C. Heath and Company
Holt	Holt, Rinehart and Winston, Inc.
Houghton	Houghton Mifflin Company
Indiana UP	Indiana University Press
Information Please	Information Please Publishing, Inc.
Johns Hopkins UP	Johns Hopkins University Press
Knopf	Alfred A. Knopf, Inc.
Larousse	Librairie Larousse
Lippincott	J. B. Lippincott Co.
Little	Little, Brown and Company
Macmillan	Macmillan Publishing Co., Inc.
McGraw	McGraw-Hill, Inc.

MIT P	Massachusetts Institute of Technology Press
MLA	Modern Language Association of America
Morrow	William Morrow and Company, Inc.
NAL	New American Library, Inc.
National Geographic Soc.	National Geographic Society
NCTE	National Council of Teachers of English
NEA	National Education Association
New Directions	New Directions Publishing Corporation
Norton	W. W. Norton and Co., Inc.
Oxford UP	Oxford University Press
Penguin	Penguin Books, Inc.
Pocket	Pocket Books
Prentice	Prentice-Hall, Inc.
Princeton UP	Princeton University Press
Putnam's	G. P. Putnam's Sons
Rand	Rand McNally and Co.
Random	Random House, Inc.
Ronald	Ronald Press
St. Martin's	St. Martin's Press, Inc.
Scott	Scott, Foresman and Co.
Scribner's	Charles Scribner's Sons
Sierra	Sierra Club Books
Simon	Simon & Schuster, Inc.
State U of New York P	State University of New York Press
Straight Arrow	Straight Arrow Publishers, Inc.
Swallow	Swallow Press
UMI	University Microfilms International
U of Chicago P	University of Chicago Press
U of Illinois P	University of Illinois Press
U of Nebraska P	University of Nebraska Press
U of New Mexico P	University of New Mexico Press
UP of Florida	University Presses of Florida
Viking	Viking Press, Inc.

Warner   Warner Books, Inc.
Yale UP   Yale University Press

Exercise   **7-2**

In order to practice composing entries for a "Works Cited" list,
complete an entry for each of the works described below. You need to
supply underlining or quotation marks around titles. I'll write the first
one for you to show you how.

1 The author of the book is Charles K. Smith.
   The title of the book is Styles and Structures: Alternative Approaches to
      Student Writing.
   It was published in 1974 by W. W. Norton and Co., Inc.

   Smith, Charles K. <u>Styles and Structures: Alternative</u>

      <u>Approaches to Student Writing</u>. New York: Norton,

      1974.

2 Author: Robin Lakoff
   Title of the book: Language and Woman's Place
   Published by Harper & Row in New York in 1975
3 Author: Max Spalter
   Title of the article: Five Examples of How to Write a Brechtian Play That
      Is Not Really Brechtian
   Periodical: Educational Theatre
   Published in the 2nd issue of 1975 on pages 220 to 235
   Note: This periodical has continuous page numbering.
4 Author: Daniel S. Greenberg
   Title of the article: Ridding American Politics of Polls
   Newspaper: Washington Post
   Published on September 16, 1980, in section A, on page 17
5 Authors: Clyde E. Blocker, Robert H. Plummer, and Richard C.
      Richardson
   Title of the book: The Two-Year College: A Social Synthesis
   Published in Englewood Cliffs, New Jersey, by Prentice-Hall in 1965
6 How would your textbook, *A Crash Course in Composition*, appear in a
   "Works Cited" list? Include the exact data.

7   In which order would the publications from 1 to 6 above appear in your list? Write the correct answer.

(a) 5 4 2 6 1 3   (b) 1 2 3 4 5 6   (c) 4 3 6 1 5 2   (d) 6 4 3 5 1 2

THE APA DOCUMENTATION STYLE FOR THE SOCIAL SCIENCES

You use the APA style this way:

A   Always mention your source and its date within the text of your paper in parentheses, like this:

> The study reveals that children pass through identifiable
>
> cognitive stages (Piaget, 1954).

B   Your readers can identify this source by consulting your References list at the end of your paper. The entry for the information above would appear like this:

> Piaget, J. (1954). The construction of reality in the child.
>   New York: Basic Books.

[Note the use of sentence capitalization for titles in the references section.]

C   If you are quoting directly or if you want to stress the authority of the source you are paraphrasing, you may mention the name of the source in your sentence. Then include just the date in parentheses, like this:

> In Words and Women, Miller and Swift (1976) remind us
>
> that using the plural is a good way to avoid "the built-in
>
> male-as-norm quality English has acquired . . ." (p. 163).

D If you are using a source written or edited by more than two people and fewer than six, cite all authors the first time you refer to the source. For all following references, cite only the surname of the first person listed, followed by "et al." (meaning "and others"):

> Blair et al. (1980) observe that the fine arts were almost
>
> ignored by colonial writers.

When there are only two authors, join their names with an "and" in the text. In parenthetical materials, tables, and reference lists, join the names by an ampersand (&).

> Hale and Sponjer (1972) originated the Do-Look-Learn
>
> theory.

> The Do-Look-Learn theory (Hale & Sponjer, 1972) was
>
> taken seriously by educators.

E If the author's name is not given, then use a shortened title instead. In your abbreviation, be sure to use at least the first word of the full title to send the reader to the proper alphabetized entry in your "References" section. The following is a reference to a newspaper article entitled "Ramifications of Baboon Use Expected to Become an Issue":

> The doctor observed that some people objected to the trans-
>
> plant on grounds that were emotional rather than rational
>
> ("Ramifications," 1979).

F If you are quoting more than *forty* words, begin the quotation on a new line and indent the entire quotation five spaces, but run each line to the usual right margin. Omit the quotation marks. Do not single-space the quotation.

In <u>Language and Woman's Place</u> (1975) Lakoff observes

that

> men tend to relegate to women things that are not of
>
> concern to them, or do not involve their egos. . . . We
>
> might rephrase this point by saying that since
>
> women are not expected to make decisions on impor-
>
> tant matters, such as what kind of job to hold, they
>
> are relegated the noncrucial decisions as a sop (p. 9).

G On your last page, a separate page, alphabetize your "References" list of all sources mentioned in your paper. Use *hanging indention:* that is, after the first line of each entry, indent the other lines five spaces.

H In your "References" section, in citing two or more works by the same author, put the earliest work first. When more than one work has been published by the same author during the same year, list them alphabetically, according to name of the book or article and identify them with an a, b, c, etc., following the date:

Graves, D. (1975). An examination of the writing
  processes of seven-year-old children. <u>Research in the</u>
  <u>Teaching of English</u> 9, 227-241.

Graves, D. (1981a). Writing research for the eighties:
  What is needed. <u>Language Arts</u>, 58, 197-206.

Graves, D. (1981b). <u>Writers: Teachers and children at</u>
  <u>work</u>. Exeter, NH: Heinemann Educational Books.

I Use the following abbreviations: Vol., No., chap., trans., ed., Ed., rev. ed., 2nd ed., p., pp. (meaning Volume, Number, chapter, translated by, edition, Editor, revised edition, second edition, page, and pages). Use official U.S. Postal Service abbreviations for states: IL, NY, TX, etc.

Sample Entries for a List of "References"

The following models will help you write entries for your "References" list for most of the sources you will use. If you use a source not treated in these samples, consult the more extensive list of sample entries found in the *Publication Manual of the American Psychological Association* or ask your instructor.

Alphabetize your list by the author's last name. If there is no author given, alphabetize the entry by the title. Use hanging indention; that is, after the first line of each entry indent the other lines five spaces.

Books and Journals

1 Book by one author:

   Abernathy, C. F. (1980). <u>Civil rights: Cases and materials.</u>

   St. Paul: West.

2 Two or more books by the same author (list in chronological order):

   Gould, S. J. (1980). <u>The mismeasure of man.</u> New York:

   Norton.

   Gould, S. J. (1981). <u>The panda's thumb: More reflections</u>

   <u>on natural history.</u> New York: Norton.

3 Book by two or more authors:

   Brusaw, C., Alfred, G. & Oliu, W. (1976). <u>The business</u>

   <u>writer's handbook.</u> New York: St. Martin's.

   Cook, M. & McHenry, R. (1978). <u>Sexual attraction.</u> New

   York: Pergamon.

[Note that in your list of references you use the ampersand sign instead of writing "and."]

4 Book by a corporate author:

White House Conference on Children and Youth. (1970).

The becoming of education. Washington, D.C.: U.S.

Government Printing Office.

5 Book with an editor:

Zaranka, W., Ed. (1981). The brand-X anthology of

poetry. Cambridge: Apple-Wood.

[For a book with two or more editors, use ''Eds.'']
6 Article in a collection or anthology:

Emig, J. (1978). Hand, eye, brain: Some basics in the

writing process. In C. Cooper & L. Odell (Eds.).

Research in composing: Points of departure (pp. 59-

72). Urbana, IL: National Council of Teachers of

English.

7 Multivolume work:

Asimov, I. (1960). The intelligent man's guide to science.

(Vols. 1-2). New York: Basic Books.

8 Later edition:

Gibaldi, J. & Achtert, W. (1984). MLA handbook for

writers of research papers (2nd ed.). New York:

MLA.

9 Article from a journal:

> Emig, J. (1977). Writing as a mode of learning. College
>
> Composition and Communication, 28, 122-128.

Other Sources

10 Personal or telephone interview, letter, lecture, etc. Not cited in Reference list, only in text citation.

11 Article from a specialized dictionary or encyclopedia. Treat as an article in a collection (number 6 above).

THE OLD MLA DOCUMENTATION STYLE

To credit borrowed material using this system, you insert consecutive note numbers (raised a half space above the line) in order to credit a source. That source is then identified with a corresponding number on a page entitled "Notes" or "Endnotes" at the end of the paper. This system would be fairly simple if we never used the same source twice. But, of course, we often do refer to a good source several times in different parts of a paper. Sometimes we quote a couple of ideas in a row from the same author. In order to avoid writing out the complete information each time, the system gives you abbreviated forms which you are expected to use. It works as shown in the following examples.

First reference to a work:

> [1]Seymour Savant, Knowledge Is Power (Philadelphia:
>
> Brotherly Love Press, 1960), p. 69.

Another reference to the same work: If you have only one author by this name in your bibliography, you simply write the last name, plus the page number, whether other notes have intervened or not:

> [4]Savant, p. 68.

If you've acquired more than one Savant, or if you're using a couple

of books by this particular Savant, you need only distinguish them by
giving a brief title after the last name for repeat entries:

⁵Savant, <u>Knowledge</u>, p. 68.

If you're quoting an unsigned article or pamphlet, you'll have no
author's name for repeat entries. Instead, abbreviate the title and cite
the page number, as shown in footnote 2 below:

¹"New Places to Look for Presidents," <u>Time</u>, Dec. 15,

1975, p. 19.

²"New Places . . . ," p. 20.

A Minor Complication   If you're quoting from an introduction,
preface, foreword, or afterword written by someone other than the
author of the main text, cite this writer's name first in the note (but not
in the bibliography). Omit quotation marks around Introd., Pref.,
Foreword, or Afterword, like this:

¹Hershel Parker, Foreword, <u>The Confidence Man</u> by

Herman Melville (New York: Norton, 1971), p. ix.

Remember also that brevity in documentation is a virtue. You are
expected to use abbreviated forms and to shorten dates and publisher's
names.

That's about all there is to it, except that different kinds of
materials (books, essays in books, encyclopedias) require different
kinds of citations. The sample entries below should cover all but the
most esoteric sources.

Sample Notes

 1   A book with one author:

¹Seymour Savant, <u>Knowledge Is Power</u> (Philadelphia:

Brotherly Love Press, 1960), p. 69.

If the author's full name is given in the text, you may use only the last name in the note. Repeat the title even if you mentioned it in the text.

2   A paperback reprint of an earlier publication:

> [2]Frederick Lewis Allen, Only Yesterday (1931, rpt.
>
> New York: Perennial-Harper, 1964), p. 28.

The abbreviation "rpt" stands for "reprinted."

3   A book with two or more authors or editors:

> [3]K. L. Knickerbocker and H. Willard Reninger, eds.,
>
> Interpreting Literature, 3rd ed. (New York: Holt, 1965), pp.
>
> 78-79.

The abbreviation "pp." stands for "pages."

4   A work in several volumes:

> [4]Albert Bigelow Paine, Mark Twain: A Biography (New
>
> York: Harper, 1912), II, 673.

Note that the abbreviation for page (or pages) is omitted when you use a volume number. This holds true for periodical entries with volume numbers also.

5   An essay in a collection, casebook, or critical edition:

> [5]William York Tindall, "The Form of Billy Budd," rpt.
>
> in Melville's "Billy Budd" and the Critics, ed. William T.
>
> Stafford (Belmont, Calif.: Wadsworth, 1961), p. 126.

6   A work in translation:

> [6]Eugene Ionesco, Rhinoceros and Other Plays, trans.
>
> Derek Prouse (New York: Grove, 1960), p. 107.

7   An anonymous article (magazine):

[7]"A Beatle Roundup," Newsweek, Sept. 7, 1970, p. 85.

8   An anonymous article (newspaper):

[8]"Smog Group to Consider Tougher Rules," Eugene

(Ore.) Register-Guard, Sept. 13, 1970, Sec. 1, p. 2, col. 3.

9   A signed article in a periodical not requiring a volume number (i.e., in a *popular*, rather than a *scholarly*, magazine):

[9]Tom Wicker, "Nixon's the One--But What?" Playboy,

Oct. 1970, p. 105.

Notice, no comma after the question mark ending the title. Don't stack up punctuation.

10   An article in a scholarly periodical requiring a volume number:

[10]Marcus Smith, "The Wall of Blackness: A Psycholog-

ical Approach to 1984," Modern Fiction Studies, 14 (Winter

1968-69), 425.

11   An unsigned encyclopedia article:

[11]"Abolitionists," Encyclopedia Americana, 1974 ed.

12   A signed encyclopedia article:

[12]T[homas] P[ar]k, "Ecology," Encyclopaedia Britan-

nica, 1968 ed.

13   An article from the *Dictionary of American Biography*:

[13]A[llan] N[evins], "Warren Gamaliel Harding," DAB

(1932).

The entry for an article from the *DNB*, the British *Dictionary of National Biography*, would be done the same way.

14 An anonymous pamphlet:

> [14]Preparing Your Dissertation for Microfilming (Ann
>
> Arbor, Mich.: University Microfilms, n.d.), p. 3.

The abbreviation "n.d." means there's no date given. Be sure to include this notation; otherwise your readers may think you carelessly omitted the date. If there are no page numbers in your pamphlet, just put a period after the parenthesis.

15 A reference to the Bible:

> [15]Amos II, 6-7.   or   [15]Amos 2:6-7.

Notice you identify only the book (Amos), the chapter (2), and the verses (6-7). Your readers are expected to recognize the source as the Bible.

16 A reference to a letter:

In a published collection:

> [16]Twain to James Redpath, Mark Twain's Letters, ed.
>
> A. B. Paine (New York: Harper, 1917), I, 190-91.

An unpublished letter:

> [16]Letter from Wharton to William Brownell, 6 Nov.
>
> 1907, Wharton Archives, Amherst College, Mass.

A personal letter:

> [16]Letter received from Gore Vidal, 2 June 1976.

17 A personal or telephone interview:

> [17]Personal interview with Ken Kesey, 28 May 1977.
>
> [17]Telephone interview with Joan Didion, 10 April 1977.

18 A review, signed or unsigned:

> [18]John Updike, "Who Wants to Know?" rev. of <u>The</u>
>
> <u>Dragons of Eden</u>, by Carl Sagan, <u>The New Yorker</u>, 22 Aug.
>
> 1977, p. 87.

> [18]Rev. of <u>Ring</u> by Jonathan Yardley, <u>The New Yorker</u>,
>
> 12 Sept. 1977, p. 159.

19 A lecture:

> [19]Rise Axelrod, "Who Did What with Whom," MLA
>
> Convention, Chicago, 30 Dec. 1977.

20 A document from ERIC:

> [20]Joseph Lucas, <u>Background for Builders</u>, Curriculum
>
> Lab (New Brunswick, N.J.: Rutgers, The State Univ., 1975),
>
> p. 6 (ERIC ED 127 459).

The "Sources Consulted" Section

English instructors now agree that there is no need to include a bibliography with a documented paper since all the information necessary for locating your sources is cited in the notes. But if you have read a number of works that you did not refer to in your paper, you might want to include a "Sources Consulted" page following your "Notes" section. Do not number the entries but *do* alphabetize them. Although the information is basically the same as in your "Notes" entries, the form is quite different, as you can see in this example:

> Kaufman, Sue. <u>Diary of a Mad Housewife</u>. New York:
>
> Random House, 1967.

1 The item is indented backwards: "hanging" instead of regular indention.

2 The last name is listed first for ease in alphabetizing.

3 The author's name is followed by a period instead of a comma.

4 The title is followed by a period instead of a parenthesis or a comma.

5 No parentheses are used, except to enclose dates for articles in periodicals using volume numbers.

6 No page numbers are listed for books.

7 Page numbers for an article or for an essay in a book indicate the length of the selection, i.e., the page on which the piece begins, followed by the page on which it ends: pp. 376–84. [With popular magazines in which articles begin at the front and are continued in the back, the only realistic solution is to give the beginning page numbers and use a plus sign (+) to indicate that there's more at the back.

8 If you should use two or more books by the same author, don't repeat the author's name. Instead, use a line, followed by a period. Then give the title and the rest of the information as usual:

Savant, Seymour. Knowledge Is Power. Philadelphia:

Brotherly Love Press, 1960.

———. Love and Its Lapses. Philadelphia: Brotherly Love

Press, 1963.

Part Two

Further Advice for Those Who Need It

Chapter 8

Revising Index

Nobody expects you to sit down and read this chapter straight through. You are expected to look up here the entries that cover whatever errors your instructor finds in your writing and correct your paper accordingly. The advice given here applies to current *standard English*, the language used by educated people in our society. While standard English is not necessarily any *better* than the language you may hear at the grocery store or in your local tavern (it may, in fact, be less vigorous and colorful), standard English is the language required of college students and in the business world. I've also included exercises so that you can get some practice on especially knotty problems.

Abbreviation   See also *Numbers.*

1 If you're writing on a formal level, you'd best not abbreviate any terms, other than the following, which are customary:

    a *Personal titles:* Mr., Ms., Mrs., Dr. Abbreviate doctor only

before the person's name: Dr. Dustbin—*but never* "The dr. removed my appendix."
St. Joan *but:* "My mother has the patience of a saint."

b *Academic degrees:* PhD., M.D., D.V.M., R.N.; or without periods: PhD, MD, DVM, RN

c *Dates or times:* 1000 B.C. or AD 150 (periods are optional here too); 10:00 a.m., 3 p.m., or 10 A.M., 3:00 P.M., *but not* "Sylvester succumbed to intoxication in the early a.m."

d *Places:* Washington, D.C. or DC, the U.S. economy, Boston, MA, *but not* "Ringo flew to the U.S. on a jumbo jet."

e *Organizations:* IRS, FBI, ITT, UNICEF, YWCA. Many organizations are commonly known by their abbreviations (usually written in capital letters without periods). If you're not certain whether your readers will recognize the abbreviation, write the name out the first time you use it, put the initials in parentheses following it, and thereafter use the initials only.

f *Latin expressions:* e.g., (for example); i.e., (that is); etc. (and so forth)—but do not use *etc.* just to avoid thinking of other examples.

g *Citations:* Most documentation styles require abbreviations; consult pages 136 to 149 for information concerning the style of the Modern Language Association.

2 Avoid using symbols (%, #, &) except in scientific papers, in which you are expected to use both numerals and symbols.

Active Voice See pages 54–56.

Adverb/Adjective Confusions

1 Most of the time you can spot an adverb by its customary *-ly* ending which is added to an adjective:

Adjective	Adverb
beautiful	beautifully
rapid	rapidly
mangy	mangily

Naturally there are exceptions—adjectives that end in *-ly* such as *sickly, earthly, homely, ghostly, holy, lively, friendly, manly*—but these

seldom cause difficulty. Also, there are adverbs that don't end in *-ly*—
now, then, later, there, near, far, very, perhaps—but hardly anybody
messes these up either.

2 The trouble stems from choosing the wrong form as a modifier.
Remember that in standard usage *adverbs* modify *verbs, adjectives,*
and other *adverbs.*

> *subj.* *vb.* *adv.*
> *Standard:* The car was vibrating badly.

> *subj.* *vb.* *adj.*
> *Faulty:* The car was vibrating bad.

> *subj.* *vb.* *adv.* *adv.*
> *Standard:* The car was moving really rapidly.

> *subj.* *vb.* *adj.* *adv.*
> *Faulty:* The car was moving real rapidly.

> *subj.* *vb.* *adv.* *adj.*
> *Standard:* The car was badly damaged.

> *subj.* *vb.* *adj.* *adj.*
> *Faulty:* The car was damaged bad.

3 *Adjectives* modify *nouns* or *pronouns:*

> *n.* *vb.* *adj.* *n.*
> Fido is a frisky pup.

> *pron.* *vb.* *adj.*
> She looks frisky.

4 *Adjectives* also follow *linking verbs (to be, to feel, to seem, to look,
to become, to smell, to sound, to taste)* and refer back to the noun or
pronoun subject:

> *subj.* *vlk.* *adj.*
> Fido feels bad.

> *subj.* *vlk.* *adj.*
> Fido smells bad.

Notice that a verb *expressing action* requires an *adverb* in what appears to be the same construction, but the adverb here modifies the verb:

> *subj.*   *vb.*⌒*adv.*
> <u>Fido</u> <u>eats</u> messily.

> *subj.*   *vb.*⌒   *adv.*
> <u>Fido</u> <u>scratches</u> frequently.

5 Some short adverbs can now be used with or without the *-ly* ending in informal writing:

Drive slowly!	Drive slow!
Yell loudly.	Yell loud.

Exercise   **8-1**

In the following sentences choose the correct form to use in writing standard English.

1 The candidate talked too (loud, loudly).
2 Onion soup tastes (delicious, deliciously).
3 Sodium nitrite reacts (dangerous, dangerously) in your stomach.
4 Drive (careful, carefully)!
5 Rhinoceroses seldom move very (quick, quickly).

Agreement (Pronoun and Antecedent)

1 Pronouns should agree in number with their antecedents. Most of the time we have no problem:

> Charlene shucked *her* sweater.

> Charlene and Susie shucked *their* sweaters.

> Neither Charlene nor Susie shucked *her* sweater!

There are some indefinite pronouns that seldom cause difficulty because they can be singular or plural, depending on the construction:

All of my money is gone.

All of my pennies are spent.

Some of this toast is burned.

Some of these peas are tasteless.

2 There are a beastly lot of *indefinite* pronouns, many of which *sound* plural but have been decreed grammatically singular:

anybody	someone
anyone	everyone
none	neither
no one	either

Consider, for instance, the logic of these grammatically correct sentences:

Since everyone at the rally spoke Spanish, I addressed him in that language.

Everyone applauded, and I was glad he did.

After everybody folded his paper, the instructor passed among him and collected it.

Robert C. Pooley points out in *The Teaching of English Usage* that grammarians since the eighteenth century have been trying to coerce writers into observing this arbitrary, often illogical, distinction.[1]

Writers—often extremely good writers—have frequently ignored the rule (italics mine):

Nobody knows what it is to lose a friend, till *they* have lost him.

—Henry Fielding

I do not mean that I think *anyone* to blame for taking due care of *their* health.

—Joseph Addison

[1](Urbana, Ill.: National Council of Teachers of English, 1946, 1974), pp. 83–87.

If a *person* is born of a gloomy temper, . . . *they* cannot help it.

—Lord Chesterfield

It's enough to drive *anyone* out of *their* senses.

—George Bernard Shaw

Nobody likes a mind quicker than *their* own.

—F. Scott Fitzgerald

Everybody must develop *their* own standards of morality.

—Dr. Mary Calderone

I firmly believe that the *person* who goes for food stamps does it because *they* are poor.

Sen. Philip Hart

The time has come to use the indefinite pronouns sensibly again, as Fielding and Addison did. Professor Pooley, in summarizing his findings on current usage, reports:

It may be concluded, then, that the indefinite pronouns *everyone, everybody, either, neither,* and so forth, when singular in meaning are referred to by a singular pronoun and when plural in meaning are referred to by a plural pronoun. When the gender is mixed [includes both females and males] or indeterminate [possibly includes both sexes] the plural forms *they, them, their* are frequently used as common gender singulars.[2]

Thus, we may now write in standard English:

Everyone should wear *their* crash helmets.

Neither of the puppies has *their* eyes open yet.

None of those arrested will admit *they* were drinking.

That takes care of what used to be a really troublesome problem with pronoun agreement. But you should realize that there are still

[2]Pooley, p. 87.

plenty of people around who will look askance at this usage. Many people who learned standard English, say, twenty years ago will declare you wrong if you write *everyone* followed by *their*. If you prefer to avoid ruffling such readers, you can simply observe the old rule and consider these pronouns as always singular: *anybody, anyone, someone, everyone, none, neither, either.* Unless you're discussing a group that's entirely female, you'll write:

> *Everyone* should wear *his* crash helmet.

> *Neither* of the informers escaped with *his* life.

> *None* of those arrested will admit *he* was drinking.

There remains, too, the sticky problem of what pronoun to use if your indefinite pronoun is strictly singular in meaning. This dilemma occurs frequently because we are programmed to write in the singular. Many people would write:

> *Each* student must show *his* permit to register.

Just as effectively, you can write:

> *Students* must show *their* permits to register.

Or, if you're fond of the singular, try this:

> *Each* student must show *a* permit to register.

The meaning remains the same and you've included both sexes. Occasionally you may need to write a sentence in which you emphasize the singular:

> *Each* individual must speak *his or her* own mind.

That usage is now quite acceptable in standard English—as long as you don't use the double pronoun very often. I favor writing that sentence this way:

> *Each one of us* must speak *our* own minds.

Try to break the singular habit and cultivate the plural. You can thus solve countless problems automatically.

Exercise   **8-2**

In the following sentences, select one or more words suitable for filling the blank in a nonsexist way. If you can't think of such a word, revise the sentence.

1 Everyone on the plane should fasten _____ seat belts.
2 All the cows were wearing _____ bells.
3 Anyone living outside of town should leave _____ job early to avoid getting _____ car stuck in a snow drift.
4 None of the cats in our house will allow _____ to be picked up.
5 Someone has left _____ car lights on.

Agreement (Subject and Verb)

1 *Agreement in number:* In standard English, subjects and verbs should agree in *number* (singular or plural):

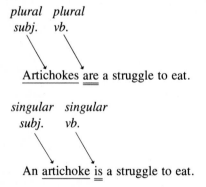

plural   plural
subj.   vb.

Artichokes are a struggle to eat.

singular   singular
subj.   vb.

An artichoke is a struggle to eat.

NOTE: The *to be* verb (*am*, *was*, *were*, etc.) agrees with the
           subject (a noun before the verb), not the predicate
           nominative (a noun following the *to be* verb).

subj.   *pr. nom.*
My favorite fruit is peaches.

subj.   *pr. nom.*
Peaches are my favorite fruit.

2 *Forming plurals:* There's one bit of confusion about plurals at the
outset. With most nouns you add an -*s* to make the plural:

snips and snails and puppydogs' tails

But with most verbs, the singular form ends in -*s* and you drop it to
form the plural.

One squirrel gnaws; several squirrels gnaw.

3 *The intervening modifier menace:* Sometimes a modifier gets
sandwiched in between subject and verb to trip the unwary, like this:

subj.   *vb.*
Wrong: The full extent of his crimes have now been discovered.

"Crimes have now been discovered" sounds fine, but *crimes* is *not*
the subject of that sentence. The actual subject is the singular noun
extent, with *crimes* serving as object of the preposition *of.* The sentence
should read:

subj.   *vb.*
Right: The full extent of his crimes has now been discovered.

Here are more correct examples of sentences with intervening
modifiers:

subj.
The boredom of minding children, cleaning floors, washing
vb.
dishes, and cooking meals has driven many women to drink.

subj.
Pictures showing nude women and men having sexual contact
vb.
are shocking.

<u>*subj.*</u>　　　　　　　　　　　*vb.*

<u>Books</u> full of adventure <u>are</u> what Lucy likes.

4 *The compound subject syndrome:* We all know that where two singular subjects are connected by *and*, we need a plural verb:

1　　+　　1　　=　　*plural*

The <u>pitcher</u> and the <u>catcher</u> <u>are</u> both big drinkers.

But sometimes we complicate matters by connecting singular subjects with *correlative conjunctions* (*not . . . but, not only . . . but also,* neither *. . . nor, either . . . or*) instead of *and.* Then the verb should be singular, although the idea may still come out plural:

Not only the pitcher but the catcher also is sloshed.

Neither the pitcher nor the catcher is sober.

Either the pitcher or the catcher is drunk.

When you use compound *plural* subjects connected by *or,* the verb should be plural:

<u>Fleas</u> or <u>ticks</u> <u>are</u> unwelcome.

If one subject is plural and the other singular, the verb agrees with the subject closest to it:

<u>Leather</u> or <u>hubcaps</u> <u>remind</u> me of you.

<u>Hubcaps</u> or <u>leather</u> <u>reminds</u> me of you.

WARNING: **Some constructions appear compound but really aren't. Singular subjects followed by words like *with, like, along with, as well as, no less than, including, besides* are still singular because these words are prepositions, not coordinating conjunctions. The *idea* in the sentence may be distinctly plural, but the subject and verb remain singular.**

My <u>cat</u>, as well as my parakeet, <u>is</u> lost.

<u>Seymour</u>, together with his St. Bernard, his pet alligator, and his piranha fish, <u>is</u> moving in with us.

<u>Claudia</u>, no less than Clyde, <u>is</u> responsible for this outrage.

5 *The verb-subject variation:* We don't always follow the usual subject-followed-by-verb sentence pattern. Always be sure of your grammatical subject and make the verb agree:

vb.   *subj.*   *vb.*
Where <u>have</u> all the <u>flowers</u> <u>gone</u>?

If the sentence is longer, you may have trouble:

> *Wrong:*   Where has all the hope, gaiety, yearning, and excitement gone?

The adverb *where* can never be the subject of a sentence, so you must look further. The actual subject is compound: "hope, gaiety, yearning, and excitement," which means the verb should be *plural*:

> *Right:*   Where <u>have</u> all the hope, gaiety, yearning, and excitement <u>gone?</u>

We often invert subject and verb for stylistic reasons:

> *Right:*   In poverty, unjustice, and discrimination <u>lies</u> the
 subj.
 <u>cause</u> of Juan's bitterness.

> *Right:*   Here <u>are</u> my friend <u>Seymour</u> and his cousin <u>Selma</u>.

Like the adverbs *here* and *where*, the word *there* often poses alluringly at the beginning of a sentence, looking for all the world like the subject. Do not be deceived. *There* can never be the subject; it's either an adverb or an *expletive* (a filler word that allows variety in sentence patterns). So before you automatically slide in a singular verb after *there*, find out what the subject really is:

$$\text{\textit{vb.}} \qquad \text{\textit{subj.}}$$

Right: There is great hope for peace today.

$$\text{\textit{vb.}} \qquad\qquad\qquad \text{\textit{subj.}}$$

Right: There are two great hopes for peace today.

The pronoun *it* can also be an expletive, but unlike *there*, it can be the subject of a sentence and always takes a singular verb, even when functioning as an expletive; thus, it causes no problem:

Right: It is a mile to the nearest phone.

Right: It is miles to the nearest phone.

6 *The collective noun option:* Some words in the language (like *group*, *staff*, *family*, *committee*, *company*, *jury*) are not decreed singular or plural. They can be either, depending upon the context. To suggest that the members are functioning together as a single unit, you can write:

The office staff is working on the problem.

Or to suggest that individual members are functioning separately within the group, you can write:

The office staff are debating that proposal.

Exercise   **8-3**

In the following sentences, choose the correct word.

1   There (is/are) Moose and Lenin, scratching furiously.
2   Where (has/have) the toothpaste and the hairbrush gone?
3   Not only Moose but Lenin also (has/have) fleas.
4   Bananas and peanut butter (make/makes) a tasty sandwich.
5   Caffeine or cigarettes, in quantity, (cause/causes) damage to the body.
6   Cigarettes or caffeine, in quantity, (cause/causes) damage to the body.
7   The impact of these statistics (has/have) not yet been fully analyzed.

8 Movies packed with violence (is/are) still a favorite with the public.
9 In great poetry (lie/lies) many great truths.
10 The jury (is/are) in disagreement about the verdict.

Analogy

An *analogy* is a form of comparison, either brief or extended. A brief analogy will be a metaphor or simile. An extended analogy provides a more thorough comparison and can be a means of organizing a paragraph, perhaps even a whole essay. You use something familiar to explain something unfamiliar. Geologists, for instance, often describe the structure of the earth's crust by comparing the strata to the layers of an onion. Sometimes writers use analogy in an attempt to persuade, as advocates of legalizing marijuana do when they argue that the present laws are as ineffective as the prohibition laws were in the twenties.

Antecedent See *Agreement* (*pronoun* and *antecedent*).

Appositive

An *appositive* is a word or phrase following a noun that renames or describes it. Appositives need commas both before and after:

> Spiny Norman, a huge hedgehog, appears on "Monty Python," a zany television series.

See also pronouns as appositives under *Case of Pronouns*, section 3.

Apostrophe

1 The apostrophe signals possession (except for the possessive pronouns, which don't need one: *ours, yours, its, theirs*):

> Clarence's kittens
>
> the Joneses' junk
>
> Yeats' yearnings

2   An apostrophe signals that some letters (or numbers) have been left out in contractions:

> we've (for *we have*)
>
> something's (for *something has* or *something is*)
>
> mustn't (for *must not*)
>
> class of '75 (for *class of 1975*)
>
> o'clock (for *of the clock*)

The chief confusion concerning apostrophes occurs with *its* and *it's*. The context of a sentence usually reveals which one you intended, but you'll mislead your readers if you carelessly choose the wrong one. So pay attention. It's easy really. Use the apostrophe only for the contraction: *It's* = it is or it has. If you use the apostrophe to form the possessive of *it* and write:

> That dumb dog chomped it's own tail.

you've really said:

> That dumb dog chomped it is own tail.

or

> That dumb dog chomped it has own tail.

And your readers may wonder about you as well as the dog. Make a mental note to check every *its* and *it's* when you proofread if you're at all careless about apostrophes.

REMEMBER: its = *of it* (possessive: **The dog chomped its tail.)**

it's = *it is* or *it has* (contraction: **It's not an intelligent dog.)**

3   An apostrophe is often optional in forming the plural of numbers, titles, letters, and words used as words:

> Clyde rolled these consecutive 7's [or 7s]. *But:* Clyde rolled three consecutive sevens.
>
> The 1970's [or 1970s] proved quieter than the 60's [or 60s].
>
> We hired two new Ph.D.'s [or PhD's].
>
> Seymour makes straight A's.
>
> Those two *and's* [or *ands*] are ineffective.
>
> You're learning the *dos* and *don'ts* of English usage.

<hr>

Exercise   **8-4**

Choose the correct word in the following sentences.
1   The (Cox's, Coxes) will be gone for two weeks.
2   That donkey is not known for (it's, its) docility.
3   The (begonias', begonias) finished blooming.
4   Some lucky (dogs', dogs) houses are as warm as toast.
5   Mind your (ps and qs, p's and q's).

<hr>

Balanced Sentence   See pages 63 to 66.

Brackets

Writers use brackets as a signal for readers in the following ways.

1   *To change verb tenses in a quotation:* Usually it's necessary to adjust your phrasing to suit a quotation, but if the quotation is past tense and you're writing in present tense (or vice versa), it's easier to change the verb in the quotation than to rewrite your paper. If you want to make a past-tense quotation about H. L. Mencken fit your present-tense essay, do it as shown in the following example.

Original in past tense:

> He defended prostitution, vivisection, Sunday sports, alcohol, and war.[3]

Changed to present tense:

> He defend[s] prostitution, vivisection, Sunday sports, alcohol, and war.[3]

2 *To clarify any word in a quotation:*

> In those days [the early 1940s] until the postwar repression set in, the [Communist] Party was a strange mixture of openness and secrecy.[4]

3 *To enclose* sic*:* When you quote a passage that contains an error, you are expected to copy the error. The word *sic* is Latin and means "thus." It means, "Honest, it really was written that way."

> The correspondent, as he rowed, looked down as [sic] the two men sleeping underfoot.[5]

4 *To enclose parenthetical material that is already within parentheses:* Use brackets this way only if you can't avoid it. It's most likely to happen in a scholarly note, like this one:

> (For an informed appraisal of her relationship with the Rev. Mr. Wadsworth, see Richard B. Sewall, *The Life of Emily Dickinson* [New York: Farrar, Straus, and Giroux, 1974], II, 444–462.)

You may not have keys for brackets on your typewriter. Do *not* substitute parentheses. If you use parentheses, your readers will assume that the material appeared in the original quotation and may become either hopelessly confused or endlessly annoyed. All you need to do is

[3]William Manchester, *H. L. Mencken, Disturber of the Peace* (New York: Collier, 1962): 79.

[4]Jessica Mitford, *A Fine Old Conflict* (New York: Knopf, 1977): 67.

[5]Stephen Crane, *The Red Badge of Courage* and *Selected Prose and Poetry*, ed. William M. Gibson, 3d ed. (New York: Holt, Rinehart and Winston, 1950): 285.

skip two spaces as you type; then write in the brackets later with a pen. Or you can make brackets with the slash and underscore keys, like this:

$$\llcorner \quad \lrcorner$$

Capitalization

1 Begin each sentence with a capital letter, including sentences you quote:

> Mark Twain observed that "It's a difference of opinion that makes a horse race."

2 Begin each line of poetry with a capital letter if the poet has used capitals:

> Candy
> Is dandy
> But liquor
> Is quicker.
>
> —Ogden Nash

> God comes in like a landlord
> and flashes on his brassy lamp.
>
> —Anne Sexton

3 Always capitalize the pronoun *I*.

4 Use caution in capitalizing words to express emphasis or personification (Truth, Justice, Beauty), unless you're writing poetry.

5 Capitalize proper nouns—the names of specific persons, places, historical events and periods, organizations, races, languages, teams, and deities.

Lowercase	Capitalized
the town square	Washington Square
go to the city	go to Boston

Lowercase	Capitalized
our club secretary	the Secretary of State
traveling east	visiting the Far East
a historical document	the Monroe Doctrine
reading medieval history	studying the Middle Ages
taking Latin, chemistry, and math	Latin 100, Chemistry 60, Math 240
an industrial town	the Industrial Revolution
a political organization	Common Cause
an ethnic group	the American Indian
our favorite team	the Galveston Gophers
buttered toast	French toast
the Greek gods	Buddha, Allah, Zeus

6 Most people capitalize pronouns referring to the Christian God or Jesus:

> Our Father, Who art in heaven, hallowed be Thy name . . . In His name, Amen.

7 When in doubt, consult your dictionary. If the word is capitalized in the dictionary entry, you should always capitalize it. If you find a usage label, like "often cap.," or "usually cap.," use your own judgment. Occasionally a word will acquire a different meaning if capitalized:

> Abraham Lincoln was a great democrat.

> Lyndon Johnson was a lifelong Democrat.

> The Pope is Catholic.

> Carla's taste is catholic (all-encompassing).

8 Capitalize the *first* and *last* words of titles; omit capitals on articles, conjunctions, and prepositions of fewer than five letters:

> *Pride and Prejudice*

> *Gone with the Wind*

> *Shakespeare Without Tears*

> *Been Down So Long It Seems like Up to Me*

> *One Flew Over the Cuckoo's Nest*

Always capitalize the first word following the colon in a title:

Problems of Urban Renewal: A Reconsideration

Case of Pronouns

1 Although nouns don't change form to show case when they move from being subjects to objects, pronouns do. We can write:

Martha resembles my sister.

My sister resembles Martha.

But with pronouns, alas, we must use a different form for subjects and objects:

She resembles my sister.

My sister resembles *her*.

The case forms are easy:

Subjective	Objective	Possessive
I	me	mine
he	him	his
she	her	hers
you	you	yours
it	it	its
we	us	ours
they	them	theirs
who	whom	whose
whoever	whomever	whosever

Most of the time the possessives give no trouble at all, except for the confusion of the possessive *its* with the contraction *it's* (see *Apostrophe*, section 2). But problems do come up like the ones in the entries which follow.

2 *When the subject or object is compound:*

Faulty: Seymour and *me* went to a lecture.

Preferred: Seymour and *I* went to a lecture.

Faulty: Martha sat with Seymour and *I.*

Preferred: Martha sat with Seymour and *me.*

If you're in doubt about which pronoun to choose, drop the noun momentarily and see how the pronoun sounds alone:

I went?   or   *me* went?

Martha sat with *me?*   or   Martha sat with *I?*

Your ear will tell you that "me went" and "sat with I" are not standard constructions.

Remember that although prepositions are usually short words (like *in*, *on*, *at*, *by*, *for*), a few are deceptively long (like *through*, *beside*, *among*, *underneath*, *between*). Long or short, prepositions always take the objective pronoun:

between Clyde and *me*

among Clyde, Martha, and *me*

beside Martha and *me*

3 *When pronouns are used as appositives:*

Faulty: *Us* cat lovers are slaves to our pets.

Preferred: *We* cat lovers are slaves to our pets.

Faulty: Spring is a delight for *we* hedonists.

Preferred: Spring is a delight for *us* hedonists.

Once more, if you're in doubt about which pronoun to choose, drop the noun and your ear will guide you: "*We* are slaves to our pets," not "*Us* are slaves to our pets"; "Spring is a delight for *us*," not "Spring is a delight for *we.*"

4 *When pronouns are used in comparisons:*

> *Faulty:*   Demon rum is stronger than *me*.
>
> *Preferred:*   Demon rum is stronger than *I*.

These comparisons are incomplete (or elliptical). If you finish the statement—at least in your mind—you'll eliminate any problem. You're not likely to write, "Demon rum is stronger than *me* am." Naturally, "stronger than *I* am" is standard English. How about "Henrietta's husband is ten years younger than *her*"? Younger than *her* is? No, younger than *she* is.

5 *When the choice is between* who *and* whom: Colloquial usage now allows *who* in all oral constructions because when we begin a sentence in conversation, we don't always know how it's going to come out.

But in writing you can always see how your sentence comes out, so you need to know whether to use *who* or *whom*. When the choice occurs in midsentence you can fall back on substitution. Replace the prospective *who* or *whom* with *she* or *her* in the following sentence, and your ear will tell you whether to choose the subjective or objective form:

> Kate Chopin was a superb writer (who/whom) literary critics have neglected until recently.

Ask yourself,

> Critics have neglected *she?*

or

> Critics have neglected *her?*

We'd all choose *her*, naturally. Since *her* is objective, the sentence needs the objective *whom:*

> Kate Chopin was a superb writer *whom* literary critics have neglected until recently.

6   There's also a sneaky way to avoid the choice. If you're writing an exam and haven't time to think, try using *that:*

> Kate Chopin was a superb writer *that* literary critics have neglected until recently.

Although many people still find this usage distasteful, it is now standard English. But don't ever substitute *which* for *who* or *whom.* Standard usage still does not allow *which* to refer to people.

Preferred:	the woman *whom* I adore
Acceptable:	the woman *that* I adore
Faulty:	the woman *which* I adore

Exercise   8-5

Choose the correct pronoun in each sentence.

1   You can't win if you run against (she/her) and Clyde.

2   At the next meeting Sherman and (I/me) are going to present a modern morality play.

3   For too long (we/us) women have been denied equality.

4   Monty Python's Flying Circus is the group on (whom/who/which) I base all hope for humor on television.

5   (Who/Whom) is going to deliver the keynote address?

6   You'll never persuade the people (who/whom/that) you need the most to go along with your proposal.

7   The very person (who/whom/that) you're trying to help is the least likely to accept your plan.

8   If you'll agree to see us tomorrow, Seymour and (I/me) will go home now.

9   Stanley and (I/me) are planning to become transcendentalists.

10 The public should be spared commercials (who/whom/that/which) are an insult to our intelligence.

Clause   See page 58.

Cliché   See page 86.

Coherence   See pages 46 to 51.

Collective Noun   See *Agreement (Subject and Verb)*, section 6.

Colon

1   Use a colon to introduce lists of things: items in a series which can be single words, phrases, or subordinate clauses.

> Joe-kitty sometimes catches small animals: birds, snakes, moles, and mice.

> It is by the goodness of God that in our country we have those three unspeakably good things: freedom of speech, freedom of conscience, and the prudence never to practice either of them.

> —Mark Twain

2   Use a colon to connect two independent clauses when the second enlarges on or explains the first:

> The students had an inspired idea: they would publish an underground newspaper.

> Only later did the truth come out: Clyde had gambled away his inheritance, embezzled the company funds, and skipped town with the loot.

If the second clause poses a question, begin with a capital letter.

> The main question is this: What are we going to do about the shortage of funds?

3 Formal usage requires a colon following a complete sentence, like this:

> My favorite animals are the following: lions, tigers, aardvarks, and hippopotamuses.

Many writers presently will insert a colon without completing the first independent clause. This usage is widely gaining acceptance.

> *Informal:*   My favorite animals are: lions, tigers, aardvarks, and hippopotamuses.

4 Use a colon (or a comma) to introduce a direct quotation:

> As Emerson observes: "Travel is a fool's paradise."

5 Use a colon to separate numerical elements:

> Time: 9:35
>
> Biblical chapter and verses: Revelations 3:7–16 *or*
>   Revelations III:7–16
>
> Act and scene: 3:2 *or* III:2
>
> Act, scene, and verse: 4:3:23–27 (*or* IV, iii, 23–27)

6 Use a colon after the salutation of a business letter:

> Dear Mr. Shuttlecock:
> Dear Service Manager:

7 Use a colon between the title and subtitle of a book or article:

> *American Humor: A Study in the National Character*
>
> "The Money Motif: Economic Implications in *Huck Finn*"

NOTE: **When typing, usually leave one space after colons, but no space in biblical references, between hours and**

minutes, and between volume and page numbers in some endnote styles (5:47–49). Leave two spaces after a colon that separates two complete sentences.

Comma   See also *Comma Splice*.

1   Use commas to set off nonessential modifiers. A word, phrase, or clause that interrupts the normal flow of the sentence without changing the meaning is nonessential or nonrestrictive. You need a comma both *before* and *after* the interrupter:

> Clarence, our cat, surprised us with three kittens.

> My father, who leads a sheltered life, took a dim view of my being arrested.

> My mother, however, saw the injustice involved.

2   Do not use commas around essential (or *restrictive*) modifiers:

> *Restrictive:*   All students who can't swim must wear life jackets on the canoe outing.

> *Nonrestrictive:*   Melvin, who can't swim, must wear a life jacket on the canoe outing.

Notice that "who can't swim" is essential to the meaning of the first example (it *restricts* the subject) but can easily be left out in the second without changing the basic meaning. Thus in the second sentence the modifier "who can't swim" is nonessential and is set off by commas. But commas around "who can't swim" in the first sentence would mislead readers. Here's another example:

> *Restrictive:*   Reservations which are not accompanied by checks will be ignored.

> *Nonrestrictive:*   Reservations, which may be submitted either by mail or by phone, will be promptly acknowledged.

3   Do not carelessly allow a *single* comma to separate subject from verb or verb from its complement:

> *Wrong:*   Minnie, being unsure of the path stopped suddenly.
>
> *Right:*   Minnie, being unsure of the path, stopped suddenly.
>
> *Wrong:*   I grabbed, without looking the wrong jacket.
>
> *Right:*   I grabbed, without looking, the wrong jacket.

4   Use a comma after any longish introductory element (like a dependent clause or a long phrase) to make the sentence easier to read:

> Before you complete your plans for vacationing in the Bahamas, you should make plane reservations.
>
> After all the trouble of sneaking into the movie, Seymour didn't like the film.

Even though commas following introductory elements are optional, use a comma if your sentence would be more difficult to read without one.

5   A comma precedes a coordinating conjunction (*and, but, or, for, nor, yet, so*) that connects two complete sentences (independent clauses):

> Myrtle splashed and swam in the pool, but Marvin only sunned himself and looked bored.

Notice, there are three coordinating conjunctions in that example, but a comma precedes only one of them. The *and's* connect compound verbs (splashed *and* swam, sunned *and* looked), not whole sentences the way the *but* does. Thus, a comma before a coordinating conjunction signals your readers that another complete sentence is coming up, not just a compound subject or object. Here are two more examples:

> Several women's rights groups are active today, yet some housewives oppose them.
>
> Clyde went to the library, so he may well be lost in the stacks.

6   Use a comma to separate two independent clauses if they are *short* and *parallel in structure*. Otherwise, you should use a semicolon.

> Heaven for climate, hell for society.
>
> > —Mark Twain

> It was the best of times, it was the worst of times. . . .
>
> > —Charles Dickens

7   Use a comma before a phrase or clause tacked on at the end of a sentence:

> The universal brotherhood of man is our most precious possession, what there is of it.
>
> > —Mark Twain

> I just failed another math exam, thanks to Rob's help at the local tavern.

NOTE: **You can use a dash instead of a comma for greater emphasis.**

> I just failed another math exam—thanks to Rob's help at the local tavern.

8   Use a comma to separate a direct quotation from your own words introducing it—if you quote a complete sentence:

> F. L. Lucas observes, ''Most style is not honest enough.''

Omit the comma if you introduce the quotation with *that* or if you quote only a part of a sentence:

> F. L. Lucas observes that ''Most style is not honest enough.''

> F. L. Lucas observes that in writing we are often ''not honest enough.''

If your introduction interrupts the quotation (as sometimes it should, for variety), you need to set off your own words with commas as you would any other interrupter:

"Most style," observes F. L. Lucas, "is not honest enough."

9   Use commas to set off nouns of direct address and other purely introductory or transitional expressions:

Direct address:

Dr. Strangelove, your proposal boggles the mind.

Your proposal, Dr. Strangelove, boggles the mind.

Your proposal boggles the mind, Dr. Strangelove.

Introductory and transitional words:

Well, anywhere you go, there you are.

My, how the child has grown.

In the first place, we must clean up the rivers.

We must, however, consider one thing first.

We must first consider one thing, however.

10   Use commas to separate elements in series:

Gertie ordered tomato juice, bacon and eggs, pancakes, and coffee with cream.

Some of the old moral values need to be revived: love, pity, compassion, honesty.

For the first sentence above, the comma before *and* is now optional. Here's another option: In the second sentence, try leaving out the commas and replacing them with *and*'s. You gain emphasis this way, but don't try it too often.

Some of the old moral values need to be revived: love and pity and compassion and honesty.

11 Use commas to separate numerals and place names and to set off names of people from titles, so they don't clump up in confusion:

> Eudora, who was born November 15, 1950, in Denver, Colorado, moved to Dallas, Texas, before she was old enough to ski.

> You may write to Laverne at 375 Fairview Avenue, Arlington, TX 20036.

> Arthur Schlesinger, Jr., writes intelligently and persuasively. Or: Arthur Schlesinger, Jr. writes intelligently and persuasively.

> The committee chose Lola Lopez, attorney-at-law, to present their case.

See also *No Punctuation Necessary* for advice about where *not* to use a comma.

Exercise   **8-6**

Try your hand at putting commas in the following sentences, if needed.

1 Your new hairstyle is stunning Seymour.
2 Oh I'll finish the job all right but it won't be because you inspired me.
3 My point however must not be misunderstood.
4 In the first place Heathcliff should never have taken the job.
5 Heathcliff should never have taken the job in the first place.
6 Although Irving takes his studies seriously he still flunks math regularly.
7 I said you made a slight miscalculation not a mistake.
8 The tall willowy red-haired girl with the short squinty-eyed bare-footed boyfriend is Jocasta.
9 Anyone who wants the most from a college education must study hard.
10 He intends to help you not hinder you.
11 The principal without a shred of evidence accused Leonard of inciting the riot.
12 If you go out please get me some cheese crackers pickles and a case of cola.
13 "Whatever you do" begged Florence "don't tell Fred."
14 Clarence had a fearful time talking his way out of that scrape yet two days later he was back in trouble again.

15 Barbara's new address is 1802 Country Club Place Los Angeles CA 90029.

Comma Splice

A comma splice (or *comma fault or comma blunder*) occurs when a comma is used to join ("splice") two independent clauses together, instead of the necessary semicolon or colon.

1 Use a semicolon or possibly a colon—*not a comma*—to separate closely related independent clauses. These sentences are correctly punctuated:

> Moose-kitty has been listless all day; he appears to have a cold.

> It's tough to tell when the cat is sick; he just lies around all day anyway.

> Tonight he skipped dinner; Moose must be sick if he misses a meal.

If you end up with comma splices, you're probably not paying attention to the structure of your sentences. You're writing complete sentences (independent clauses) without realizing it.

2 There's another devilish complication, though, that can produce comma splices. Conjunctive adverbs—transitional words like *indeed*, *therefore*, *nevertheless*, *however*—sound for all the world like coordinating conjunctions, but they are not. They cannot connect two independent clauses with only a comma the way coordinating conjunctions can. The solution to this seemingly baffling difficulty is to memorize the coordinating conjunctions: *and*, *but*, *or*, *for*, *nor*, *yet*, *so*. Then all you have to do is remember that all those other words that sound like pure conjunctions really aren't; hence with the others you need a semicolon:

> It's tough to tell when the cat is sick; indeed, he just lies around all day anyway.

3 One final word of warning: Try not to confuse the conjunctive adverbs (listed on page 224) with subordinating conjunctions (listed on page 203). A subordinating conjunction at the beginning of a clause produces a *dependent*, not an independent, clause. Thus, you don't need a semicolon in the following sentence because there's only one independent clause:

> It's tough to tell when the cat is sick, because he just lies around all day anyway.

If you know you have difficulty with comma splices, slip a bookmark into your textbook to mark the list at page 224, and another at page 203. Get into the habit of checking your punctuation when you revise.

4 *Remember* that independent clauses (except short, balanced ones) must be separated by something stronger than a comma. You have all these options:

a *Use a semicolon:*

> Moose-kitty feels better today; he's outside chasing the neighbor's dog.

b *Use a period:*

> Moose-kitty feels better today. He's outside chasing the neighbor's dog.

c *Use subordination to eliminate one independent clause:*

> Moose-kitty apparently feels better today, since he's out chasing the neighbor's dog.

d *Use a comma plus a coordinating conjunction:*

> Moose-kitty feels better today, so he's outside chasing the neighbor's dog.

e *Use a semicolon plus a conjunctive adverb:*

> Moose-kitty feels better today; indeed, he's out chasing the neighbor's dog.

Exercise   **8-7**

Correct any comma splices in the following sentences. Just to increase the challenge, I've included one that is already correct.

1 We just passed Clark Kent, he was changing his clothes in a telephone booth.
2 Doris says she doesn't want to live on a cannibal isle, she'd be bored.
3 Once a week I go out into the country and fill my lungs with clean air, this outing gives me a chance to remember what breathing used to be like.
4 Henrietta spent a grim half-hour shampooing Bowser to get rid of fleas, Bowser probably preferred to keep them.
5 Hunched over her typewriter, Flossie doggedly pecks out her term paper, it isn't even due until Monday.
6 Clyde complains that his history class offers little intellectual challenge, yet he never even reads the textbook.
7 This paper is due at nine o'clock in the morning, thus you'll have to go to the movies without me.
8 You can't control your temper, Throckmorton, you shouldn't be teaching a Carnegie course.
9 Seymour's a polite young man, as far as I know, he never swears.
10 My opinion of Orville is not high, because he has a closed mind, I doubt that he'll be a good teacher.

Comparisons, Incomplete or Illogical

1 If you're going to draw a comparison, be sure that you mention at least two things being compared:

Incomplete:	Seymour has the nicest manners.
Improved:	Seymour has the nicest manners of anyone I know.
Incomplete:	Eloise has fewer inhibitions.
Improved:	Eloise has fewer inhibitions now that she's Maybelle's roommate.
Improved:	Eloise has fewer inhibitions than Maybelle.

2 Be sure that the second element of your comparison is not ambiguous or vague. See *Predication, Faulty.*

3 Do not compare words that denote absolutes, like *unique, omnipotent, infinite, perfect, outstanding.*

> *Illogical:*   Russell came up with a very unique design.
>
> *Improved:*   Russell came up with a unique design.

Conciseness See pages 78 to 79.

Concrete Examples See pages 45 to 46.

Confused Sentence See pages 68 to 70.

Conjunctions, Coordinating See *Comma Splice*, section 2.

Conjunctions, Correlative See *Agreement (Subject and Verb)*, section 4.

Conjunctions, Subordinating See *Comma Splice*, section 2, and *Comma*, section 3. For a list of subordinating conjunctions, see *Fragment*, section 2.

Conjunctive Adverb See *Semicolon*, sections 2 to 4, and *Comma Splice*, section 2.

Connotation and Denotation See pages 93 to 95.

Contraction See *Apostrophe*, section 2.

Coordinating Conjunction See *Comma Splice*, section 2.

Correlative Conjunction See *Agreement (Subject and Verb)*, section 4.

Dangling Modifier

A modifier is a word, a phrase, or a clause that describes, qualifies, or in some way limits another word in the sentence.

1 Be sure every modifier in a sentence actually has a word to modify; otherwise, it will be a *dangling modifier*:

Dangling:	Staring in disbelief, the car jumped the curb and crashed into a telephone booth.
Improved:	While I stared in disbelief, the car jumped the curb and crashed into a telephone booth.
Dangling:	When only seven years old, her father ran off with another woman.
Improved:	When Marcella was only seven years old, her father ran off with another woman.

2 Unwise use of the passive voice often causes dangling modifiers. (In the last example below, *you* is understood as the subject of both *pin* and *cut*.)

Dangling:	After carefully pinning on the pattern, the material may then be cut.
Improved:	After carefully pinning on the pattern, you may then cut the material.
Improved:	First pin on the pattern; then cut the material.

In order to avoid dangling modifiers, you must think carefully about what you're writing. You can eliminate many of your modifier problems by writing consistently in the active voice: "I made a mistake," rather than "A mistake was made."

See also *Misplaced Modifier*.

EXERCISE   **8-8**

Identify any dangling modifiers in the following sentences, and then revise to eliminate the problem.

1 After subduing the protesters, the meeting resumed.
2 Driving through the lush, pine-scented forest, the air was suddenly fouled by the sulfurous belchings of a paper mill.
3 After bolting down lunch and racing madly to the station, the train left without us.
4 Looking back in history, Americans have often professed individualism while rewarding conformity.
5 To avoid hitting the bumper of the car in front, the pedestrian was struck.

Dash

The dash—which requires your readers to pause—is more forceful than a comma. You can use dashes to gain emphasis, as long as you use them sparingly.

1 Use a dash to add emphasis to an idea at the end of a sentence:

Emphatic:	Maybelle had only one chance—and a slim one at that.
Less emphatic:	Maybelle had only one chance, and a slim one at that.

2 Use dashes, instead of commas, around an interrupter to emphasize the interrupting material. To take away emphasis from an interrupter, use parentheses:

Emphatic:	My cousin Clyde—the crazy one from Kankakee—is running for the legislature.
Less emphatic:	My cousin Clyde, the crazy one from Kankakee, is running for the legislature.
Not emphatic:	My cousin Clyde (the crazy one from Kankakee) is running for the legislature.

3 Use dashes around an interrupter if commas appear in the interrupting material:

All the dogs—Spot, Bowser, Fido, and even Old Blue—have gone camping with Clyde.

4 Use a dash (or a colon, if you want to be more formal) following a series at the beginning of a sentence:

> Patience, sympathy endurance, selflessness—these are what good mothers are made of.

NOTE: **Do not confuse the dash with the hyphen. On your typewriter, strike *two* hyphens to make a dash. To use a hyphen when you need a dash is a serious mistake; hyphens connect, dashes separate.**

Diction   See pages 71 to 87.

Ellipsis Dots

1 Use three dots to show your readers that you've omitted words from a direct quotation:

a   *Something left out at the beginning:*

> About advice, Lord Chesterfield wrote, ". . . Those who want it the most always like it the least."

> —Letter to his son, 1748

b   *Something left out in the middle:*

> "The time has come . . . for us to examine ourselves," warns James Baldwin, "but we can only do this if we are willing to free ourselves from the myth of America and try to find out what is really happening here."

> —*Nobody Knows My Name*

c   *Something left out at the end:*

> Thoreau declared that he received only one or two letters in his life "that were worth the postage" and observed summarily that "to a philosopher all *news*, as it is called, is gossip. . . ."

> —*Walden*, Chapter 2

NOTE: **The extra dot is the period.**

NOTE ALSO: **An omission which changes the meaning—even though you alert your reader with ellipsis dots— is misleading and dishonest. You should omit from quotations only portions that do not alter the meaning.**

2 If you're quoting only a snatch of something—and your readers can *tell* you're doing so—do not use ellipsis dots:

> Occasionally, like Eliot's Prufrock, we long to be "scuttling across the floors of silent seas."

3 Use either ellipsis dots or a dash to indicate an unfinished statement, especially in recording conversation:

> "But, I don't know whether . . . ," Bernice began.
>
> "How could you—?" Ferdinand faltered.

Elliptical Construction   See *Case of Pronouns*, section 4.

Emphasis   See pages 61 to 64; 65 to 66; 80.

Exclamation Point   See also *Quotation Marks*, section 8.

1 Do not use exclamation points merely to give punch to ordinary sentences. Write a good, emphatic sentence instead:

> *Ineffective:*   LeRoy was in a terrible accident!
>
> *Improved:*   LeRoy, whose motorcycle collided with a semi on US 51, lies near death from head injuries.

2 Use exclamation points following genuine exclamations:

> O kind missionary, O compassionate missionary, leave China! Come home and convert these Christians!
>
> —Mark Twain, "The United States of Lyncherdom"

> I'm mad as hell, and I'm not going to take it anymore!
>
> —Paddy Chayefsky, *Network*

NOTE: **Never stack up punctuation. Do not put a comma after an exclamation point or after a question mark.**

Expletive

1 An *expletive* can be an oath or exclamation, often profane. You'll have no trouble thinking of the four-letter ones, so I'll mention some socially acceptable ones: Thunderation! Tarnation! Oh, drat! Darn! Oh, fudge!

2 The words *it* and *there* are also expletives, but of a different sort. These expletives serve as filler words to allow for variety in sentence patterns:

> *It* is raining.

> *There* are two ways to solve the problem.

Remember that you won't achieve variety if you begin more than an occasional sentence this way; instead, you'll get wordiness.

See also *Agreement (Subject and Verb)*, section 5.

Figures of Speech   See pages 86 to 87.

Formal Usage   See pages 72 to 73.

Fragment

1 A sentence fragment, as the term suggests, is only part of a sentence but is punctuated as a whole. Many accomplished writers use fragments for emphasis, or simply for convenience, as in the portions italicized in the following examples:

> Man is the only animal that blushes. *Or needs to.*

> —Mark Twain

> I did not whisper excitedly about my Boyfriends. *For the best of reasons.* I did not have any.

> —Gwendolyn Brooks

No member [of Congress] had ever been challenged or even questioned about taking the exemption. Until my nomination.

—Geraldine Ferraro

If there is to be a new etiquette, it ought to be based on honest, mutual respect and responsiveness to each other's real needs. *Regardless of sex.*

—Lois Gould

She did not suffer any pain, and that is true—if imprisonment is not pain. *While she demanded our love in every way she knew, without sense of shame, as a child will.*

—Alice Munro

2 Avoid fragments in formal writing (term papers, business reports, scholarly essays):

Fragment: Pollution poses a serious problem. *Which we had better solve.*

Complete: Pollution poses a serious problem—which we had better solve.

Complete: Pollution poses a serious problem, which we had better solve.

NOTE: **If you write fragments accidentally, remember that a simple sentence beginning with one of the following subordinating words will come out as a fragment:**

after	since	unless
although	so as	until
as, as if	as far as	when
because	so that	whenever
before	still	whereas
if	through	which
only	till	while

Fragment: Although I warned him time after time.

Complete: I warned him time after time.

Complete: Although I warned him time after time, Clyde continued to curse and swear.

NOTE: **Words ending in *-ing* and *-ed* can cause fragments also. Although such words sound like verbs, sometimes they're verbals—actually nouns or adjectives. Every complete sentence requires an honest-to-goodness verb.**

Fragment: Singing and skipping along the beach.

Complete: Juan went singing and skipping along the beach.

Fragment: Abandoned by friends and family alike.

Complete: Alice was abandoned by friends and family alike.

Complete: Abandoned by friends and family alike, Alice at last recognized the evils of alcohol.

4 Fragments are fine in asking and answering questions, even in formal writing:

When should the reform begin? At once.

How? By throwing the scoundrels out of office.

Fragments are also necessary for reproducing conversation, since people don't always speak in complete sentences. Mark Twain records this conversation he supposedly had with his mother:

"I suppose that during all [my sickly childhood] you were uneasy about me?"
"Yes, the whole time."
"Afraid I wouldn't live?"
After a reflective pause, ostensibly to think out the facts.
"No—afraid you would."

—Mark Twain, *Autobiography*

5 When you connect two sentences with a semicolon, be sure that both constructions really are sentences:

Questionable:	He looked a lot like Quasimodo; although I couldn't see him too well.
Improved:	He looked a lot like Quasimodo, although I couldn't see him too well.
Improved:	He looked a lot like Quasimodo; I couldn't see him too well though.

Exercise   **8-9**

Some of the following constructions are not complete sentences. Correct the ones that you consider faulty. Defend the ones that you find effective.

1 Marion was late to his own wedding. To his eternal sorrow.
2 Broadcasting moment-by-moment, hour-by-hour, day-by-day reports.
3 Because she is allergic to fleas and scratches her skin raw. Our little dog needs regular bathing.
4 What is the best policy? To do nothing—diplomatically.
5 Rosita passed her exams. By studying twelve hours a day.

Fused Sentence   See *Run-On Sentence*

Hyphen

Unlike exclamation points, hyphens are much in fashion today as a stylistic device.

1 Writers sometimes hyphenate clichés (to revitalize them) or descriptive phrases that are used as a whole to modify a noun:

Emily Dickinson challenges the time-heals-all-wounds adage.

Women today are pressing for equal-pay-for-equal-work laws.

2 Hyphenate compound adjectives when they come before the noun:

a feather-light touch

high-speed railroads

But if the descriptive phrase comes after the noun, omit the hyphen:

a touch light as a feather

railroads running at high speed

3 Most compound words beginning with *self-* and *ex-* are hyphenated:

self-employed   ex-wife

self-deluded   ex-slave

self-abuse   ex-President

Never use a hyphen in the following words:

yourself	himself	itself
themselves	herself	selfless
ourselves	myself	selfish
oneself (or one's self)		

4 Consult your dictionary about other compound words. Some words change function depending on whether they're written as one word or two:

Verb: Where did I *slip up?*

Noun: I made a *slipup* somewhere.

5 Use a hyphen to divide words at the end of a line. *Divide only between syllables.* Consult your dictionary if in doubt.

NOTE: **In typing, do not leave a space either before or after a hyphen.**

Incomplete Comparisons   See *Comparisons, Incomplete and Illogical*

Linking Verb

Linking verbs do just what the term implies. They connect the subject of the sentence with the complement. The most common linking (or copulative, as they used to be bluntly called) verbs are these: *to be, to feel, to appear, to seem, to look, to smell, to sound, to taste.* See also *Adverb/Adjective Confusion*, section 4.

Misplaced Modifier

Keep modifiers close to what they modify (describe, limit, or qualify).

Faulty:	Once married, the church considers that a couple has signed up for a lifetime contract.
Improved:	The church considers that a couple, once married, has signed up for a lifetime contract.
Faulty:	I had been driving for forty years when I fell asleep at the wheel and had an accident.

Improved: Although I had driven safely for forty years, last
                 night I fell asleep at the wheel and had an accident.

Exercise   **8-10**

In the following sentences move any misplaced modifiers so that the
statements make better sense.

1 Also soft and cuddly, the main appeal of a kitten is its playfulness.
2 Registration assignments will not be accepted from students until the door
   attendant has punched them.
3 Although similar in detail, my purpose is to show how these two pussycats
   differ.
4 I was sure the old fellow even before I hit him would never make it across
   the street.
5 Clyde was robbed at gunpoint in an elevator where he lives.

Modifiers

The numerous ways of placing modifiers allows almost infinite variety
in the English sentence. For a quick run-down of several of these
methods, see *Adjective/Adverb*; *Appositives*; *Comma*, sections 1, 3,
and 6; *Dash*; and *Sentence Combining*, pages 58 to 60.

For several ways in which modifiers are often misused, see
Dangling Modifier, *Misplaced Modifier*, and *Squinting Modifier*.

Mood   See *Subjunctive Mood*.

Nonrestrictive Clause   See *Comma*, section 1.

No Paragraph

If your instructor marks ''no ¶'' on your paper, you have indented
needlessly. Journalists tend to indent every two or three sentences for
easy readability in narrow news columns, but in an essay or a report,
that much indenting produces choppy paragraphing. You should start

a new paragraph when you finish developing one idea and move on to the next.

Usually, you can correct choppy paragraphing by simply combining two or more paragraphs, like these written by a student:

> One positive effect of legalization is that marijuana would be safer to use. There would be none of this intervention from the Mafia that introduces poisons into the product before it is sold. ↫
>
> *no ¶* ⊂ Smokers would be assured of good quality marijuana because competition would arise among the producers. There wouldn't be any additives, such as "angel dust," which can have a bad effect on some people.

Certainly there was no need for the new paragraph, since the first sentence (the topic sentence) is broad enough to include the ideas in both paragraphs.

No Punctuation Necessary

If you are a comma fancier, you may be in the habit of inserting commas wherever you would pause in speaking. That practice doesn't always work; we pause far too often in speech, and different speakers pause in different places. Here are some situations that seem particularly tempting to comma abusers.

1 *When main sentence parts are long:* Some writers mistakenly separate the subject from the verb or the verb from the complement, like this:

> *Wrong:* Tall people with quick reflexes, make particularly good basketball players.
>
> *Wrong:* By the end of the year we all understood, that using too many commas would make us grow hair on our palms.

Neither of those sentences should have a comma in it. In the second sentence the clause is restrictive (it serves as the direct object of the verb *understood*) and thus should not be set off with a comma.

2   *When a restrictive clause occurs in midsentence:* Putting a comma on one end of a clause and no punctuation at all on the other end is never correct. Nonrestrictive clauses always need punctuation on both ends (see *Comma*, section 1), and restrictive ones need no punctuation. Avoid errors like this one:

> *Wrong:*   Ruthie's poem that described the death of her husband,
>   was the most moving one she read.

No comma is necessary in that sentence.

3.   *When the word* and *appears in the sentence:* Some people always put a comma before the word *and*, and they're probably right more than half the time. It's correct to put a comma before *and* when it joins the last word in a series or when it joins independent clauses. But when *and* doesn't do either of those things, a comma before it is inappropriate. This sentence, for instance, should have no comma:

> *Wrong:*   Mark called the telephone company to complain about
>   his bill, and got put on "hold" for an hour.

Numbers

Spell out the numbers one hundred and under. In general, write numbers over one hundred in figures. Spell out round numbers requiring only a couple of words (two hundred tons, five thousand dollars). If a series of numbers occurs in a passage, and some of them are over one hundred, use figures for all of them. You should also always use figures for addresses (27 White's Place), for times (1:05 P.M.), for dates (October 12, 1950), and for decimals, code and serial numbers, percentages, measurements, and page references.

EXCEPTION: **Never begin a sentence with a numeral; spell it out or rewrite the sentence.**

Paragraph

The proofreader's mark ¶ means that your instructor thinks you should indent to begin a new paragraph at that point. When all your sentences are closely related, sometimes you forget to give your readers a break by dividing paragraphs.

Remember to indent when you shift topics or shift aspects of a topic. For instance, look at the break between the preceding paragraph and this one. Both of these paragraphs are on the same subject (paragraphing), but the topic shifts from *why* to begin a new paragraph to *when* to begin a new paragraph. Hence, the indentation.

See also *No Paragraph* and *Unity.*

Parallel Structure   See pages 63 to 66.

Parentheses

1 Use parentheses around parts of a sentence or paragraph that you would speak aloud as an aside—a slight digression or some incidental information that you don't particularly want to emphasize:

> John Stuart Mill (1806–1873) promoted the idea of woman's equality with men.

> Russell's lapses of memory (often he forgets what he went to the store to buy) are probably caused by his inability to concentrate.

2 Sometimes you'll choose parentheses to separate a part of a sentence that could be enclosed in commas, as in the example above (about Russell's memory lapses). Use commas to separate material that is directly relevant to the main passage, and parentheses to separate material that is indirectly related or less crucial. When you use dashes around a part of a sentence, they strongly stress that part, as neither commas nor parentheses do.

3 Use parentheses around numerals when you number a list:

> Her professor did three things that bothered her: (1) He called her "honey," even though he didn't know her; (2) he graded the class on a curve, even though there were only ten students; (3) he complained that male students no longer wore suitcoats and ties to class.

4 Punctuation goes inside the parentheses if it punctuates just the words inside:

> Consumers can use their power by boycotting a product. (The word *boycott* is from Captain Charles C. Boycott, whose neighbors in Ireland ostracized him in 1880 for refusing to reduce the high rents he charged.)

5 Punctuation goes outside the parentheses if it punctuates more than just the enclosed material. A numbered list, like that in section 3, is the *only* case in which you would put a comma, semicolon, colon, or dash before an opening parenthesis.

Exercise   **8-11**

Choose the best punctuation (parentheses, dashes, or commas) to put in place of the carats in the following sentences. Remember: Dashes *stress*, parentheses *play down*, and commas *separate* for clarity.

1 The 1960 *World Book Encyclopedia* claims that smoking marijuana ∧*cannabis sativa*∧ causes fits of violence.
2 I tasted his omelette and found∧how disgusting!∧that it was runny inside.
3 Stewart Alsop∧whom my mother claims as a distant relation of ours∧was a well-known conservative journalist.
4 People often mistakenly think that Lenin∧our black and white cat∧was named after John Lennon of the Beatles.
5 Alcohol∧although a dangerous drug∧is considered harmless by many Americans.

Participle   See *Tense*.

Passive Voice   See pages 54 to 57.

Period

Use a period at the end of a complete declarative sentence and after most abbreviations (see *Abbreviations*). If a sentence ends with an abbreviation, let its period serve as the final period of the sentence: don't double up.

Phrase

A phrase is a group of words that does not include a subject and verb combination.

Point of View   See *Shifts in Tense and Person.*

Possessives   See *Apostrophe* and *Case of Pronouns.*

Possessives with Gerunds

1   A gerund is a verb with an *-ing* on it that acts like a noun in a sentence:

> Squishing mud between your toes is a sensual pleasure.

Squishing is the subject of the sentence and thus acts like a noun.

> He got back at the telephone company by folding his computer billing card each month.

Folding is the object of the preposition and thus acts like a noun.

2   In formal writing, you should use possessive nouns and pronouns before gerunds because gerunds act as nouns. You probably wouldn't forget to use a possessive before a regular noun in a sentence like this:

> I worry about Teddy's impulsiveness.

But people often forget to use the possessive before a gerund.

Colloquial:	I worry about *Teddy* getting lost.
Formal:	I worry about *Teddy's* getting lost.
Colloquial:	I worry about *him* getting lost.

Formal: I worry about *his* getting lost.

Predication, Faulty

1 This error comes from shifting your thought slightly in midsentence and then not rereading carefully enough to notice the problem. A sentence with faulty predication is one whose predicate doesn't match the subject in meaning:

> *Faulty:* Your first big city is an event that changes your whole outlook if you grew up in a small town.

> *Faulty:* The importance of graceful hip movement is essential when doing the Bump.

> *Faulty:* Smoothness and precision are among the basic problems encountered by beginning dancers.

In the first sentence, a city is not really an event; in the next, the writer probably didn't want to say something as banal as "importance is essential"; and in the last, smoothness and precision are not problems.

To correct such errors, you can revise the subject, the predicate, or both to make them match up better. Here are possible revisions of those problem sentences:

> *Improved:* Your first visit to a big city is an experience that changes your whole outlook if you grew up in a small town.

> *Improved:* Graceful hip movement is essential when doing the Bump.

> *Improved:* Roughness and imprecision are among the weaknesses of beginning dancers.

2 Your predication can be merely weak instead of utterly illogical. Important words should appear as the subject and predicate:

> *Weak:* One important point of his speech was the part in which he stressed self-reliance.

In the example above, the key subject and predicate words are *point
. . . was . . . part*, which don't carry much meaning in the sentence.
Here's an improvement:

> *Improved:*   At one important point, his speech emphasized self-
> reliance.

Now the key subject and predicate words are *speech . . . emphasized
. . . self-reliance*, which are more meaningful.

Preposition Problems

Explaining when to use which preposition or when to leave one out is
next to impossible. But standard English doesn't allow constructions
like these:

> *Colloquial:*   Tyrone did as good of a job as he could.
>
> *Colloquial:*   This is the kind of an example I mean.

If you write sentences like these, you need to find a friend to point out
your surplus words. Those sentences should read like this:

> *Standard:*   Tyrone did as good a job as he could.
>
> *Improved:*   Tyrone did the best job he could.
>
> *Standard:*   This is the kind of example I mean.

Prepositions, Redundant

Avoid using a preposition at the end of any sentence involving *where*:

> *Colloquial:*   Can you tell me where the action's at?
>
> *Standard:*   Can you tell me where the action is?
>
> *Colloquial:*   Where is our money going to?
>
> *Standard:*   Where is our money going?

Pronouns

Pronouns, those words that take the place of nouns, have numerous useful functions but can also cause trouble in devilish ways. See *Agreement (Pronoun and Antecedent)*; *Case of Pronouns*; pronouns for coherence, page 51; *Indefinite "You,"* page 53; *Reference of Pronouns (this* and *which* especially); *Shifts in Person*; in the "Glossary of Usage": *he or she/his or her*; *its/it's*; *their/there/they're*; *who/which/ that*; *you (indefinite)*; *your/you're*.

Proper Noun

A common noun names a class (like *dog, city*); a proper noun names a specific person, place, or thing (like *Rover, Chicago*).

Qualification   See page 99.

Quotation Marks

See also *Comma*, section 7 and pages 116 to 118 in the researched writing chapter.

1   *Quotation marks should appear around words that you copy just as they were written or spoken, whether they are complete or partial sentences:*

> "Gloria, please don't practice your quacky duck imitation while I'm trying to do my income tax," Susie pleaded.

> She said that Gloria's barnyard imitation made her "feel like moving to New York for some peace and quiet."

2   *A quotation within a quotation should have single quotation marks around it:*

> I remarked, "I've disliked Melvin ever since he said I was 'a typical product of the Midwest.'"

Don't panic if you read a book or article that reverses double and single quotation marks (that is, uses single around quotations and double around quotations within quotations). The British do it the opposite of the American way, so that book or article is probably British.

3 *If you paraphrase* (i.e., change words from the way they were written or spoken), *you're using indirect quotation and should not use quotation marks:*

Susie observed that Gloria's pig grunt was particularly disgusting.

Her actual words were, "Gloria's pig grunt is the worst of all."

Melvin told me that he despised levity.

He actually said, "I despise levity."

4 *When you write dialogue* (*conversation between two or more people*), *give each new speaker a new paragraph. But still put related nondialogue sentences in the same paragraph:*

After our visitor finally left, I was able to ask my question. "What did he mean by calling me 'a typical product of the Midwest'?" I inquired.

"Maybe he meant you were sweet and innocent," Michele suggested.

"Fat chance," I replied. "He probably meant I was corny."

5 *Put quotation marks around titles of works that you think of as* part *of a book or magazine rather than a whole by itself: articles, stories, chapters, essays, short poems. Do not, however, put quotation marks around titles of your own essays.*

"Petrified Man," a short story by Eudora Welty

"We Real Cool," a poem by Gwendolyn Brooks

"My View of History," an essay of Arnold Toynbee

Underline the titles of works you think of as a whole: *books, magazines, journals, newspapers, plays, and movies* (Walden, The

New York Times, Casablanca). *Also underline the names of works of visual art* (Dali's painting, Civil War). Italics in print mean the same thing as underlining by hand or on a typewriter.

6 *Underline or put quotation marks around words used as words*, but be consistent once you decide which method to use in a paper.

You used *but* and *and* too often in that sentence.

He thought "sophisticated" only referred to stylishness.

7 *In general, don't put quotation marks around words that you suspect are too slangy.* It's tempting to do this:

Weak: Phys ed was really a "drag."

Weak: On the first day of class, my philosophy instructor showed that he was really "hot" on the subject.

But you should take the time to decide whether the informality of the slang suits your audience and purpose. If it does, there's no need to set it off with quotation marks. If it doesn't, you should find a more fitting expression. In the first example, since the writer used the slangy, abbreviated form of physical education, the informal word *drag* is suitable without any quotation marks. In the second example, the writer should probably substitute *enthusiastic about* for "*hot on*."

Don't use quotation marks as a written sneer, either. Learn to express your distaste in a more precise and effective way.

8 *Periods and commas always go inside quotation marks:*

"Never eat at a restaurant named Mom's," my brother always said.

In James Joyce's story "Eveline," the main character is at once frightened and attracted by freedom.

When a quoted sentence is followed by tag words (like *he whined*, *she said*, *Gloria grunted*), substitute a comma for the period at the end of the quoted sentence. When the tag words interrupt a quoted sentence, the first part of the quotation needs a comma after it:

"I must admit," Seymour said, "that Gloria sounds more like a rooster than anyone else I know."

9 *Colons, semicolons, and dashes always go outside the quotation marks:*

"If at first you don't succeed, try, try again"; "It takes all kinds"; "You can't get something for nothing": these shallow mottos were his entire philosophy of life.

10 *Exclamation points and question marks go inside the quotation marks if they are part of the quotation and outside if they are not:*

"That man called me 'Babycakes'!" Sandra screeched.

He said, "Hey there, Babycakes, whatcha doin' tonight?"

Isn't that what my father calls "an ungentlemanly advance"?

11 *Do not use quotation marks to indicate sarcasm or a verbal sneer,* like this:

Wrong: The new income tax reform is the "best thing" that Washington has come up with in years.

Instead, make the sarcasm clear without quotation marks, like this:

Right: The new income tax reform is the best thing that Washington has come up with since giving us the Great Depression of the 1930s.

Or else, eliminate the sarcasm, like this:

Right: The new income tax reform is the most disastrous thing Washington has come up with in years.

Exercise   **8-12**

Add single or double quotation marks to these items.

1 Did you see the article Dietmania in *Newsweek*? she asked.

2 He called Gloria's performance an embarrassment to man and beast.
3 Until I heard Gloria, I though that oink was the basic pig sound.
4 At first, Gloria said, I just did easy ones like ducks and lambs.
5 In March she mourned, I will never get the emu call right; however, by May she had learned it perfectly.

Redundant Prepositions See *Prepositions, Redundant.*

Reference of Pronouns

1 Pronouns are useful words that stand in for nouns so that we don't have to be forever repeating the same word. Occasionally pronouns cause trouble, though, when readers can't tell for sure *what* noun the pronoun stands for (or refers to). If, for instance, you write:

> Seymour gave Selma her pet parrot.

There's no problem: *her* clearly means Selma. But suppose you write instead:

> Seymour gave Clyde his pet parrot.

Instant ambiguity: *his* could mean either Seymour's or Clyde's. In order to avoid baffling your readers in this fashion, you should rephrase such constructions in a way that makes the pronoun reference clear:

> Seymour gave his pet parrot to Clyde.

or

> Clyde got his pet parrot from Seymour.

If you have difficulty with vague pronoun reference, start checking pronouns when you proofread. Be sure each pronoun refers clearly to only *one* noun. And be sure that noun is fairly close, preferably in the same sentence. You cannot expect your readers to track back two or three sentences to find the antecedent for a pronoun.

2 Use *this* and *which* with care. Whenever you use the word *this*, try to follow it with a noun telling what *this* refers to. We're naturally lazy and take advantage of such a handy word, which can be a pronoun and stand there by all by itself meaning nothing in particular. Naturally, *this* will mean something to *you* when you write it, but you must be sure that the idea also gets onto the page. Too often *this* refers to an abstract idea or to a whole cluster of ideas in a paragraph, and your readers would require divine guidance to figure out exactly what you had in mind. So, if you're going to write:

> The importance of this becomes clear when we understand the alternatives.

at least give your reader a clue: "this *principle*," "this *qualification*," "this *stalemate*" or even "this *problem*," if you can't pinpoint the meaning any better than that. It takes extra time and energy to think of the right word, even though you may know exactly what you mean. But searching for a single word to express the idea will help your readers understand you.

Which causes similar problems. Often this handy pronoun refers to the entire clause preceding it. Sometimes the meaning is clear, sometimes not. Suppose you write:

> Jocasta has received only one job offer, which depresses her.

That sentence can be interpreted in two different ways:

> Jocasta is depressed about receiving only one job offer, even though it's a fairly good job.

or

> Jocasta has received only one job offer—a depressing one, at that.

Remember that such ambiguity is undesirable in expository prose. Check every *this* and *which* to be sure your readers will understand these words to mean exactly what you intended.

Look up *Agreement* (*Pronoun and Antecedent*) for a discussion of more pronoun problems.

3 The word *it* can be an *expletive*, a filler word that delays the subject and has no precise meaning:

> Since *it* has rained for ten days straight, *it* looks as if we should start building an ark.

But often *it* is a pronoun and needs a clear antecedent:

> *Unclear:*   The campaign is over and the election starts today. Sometimes *it* is exciting.

Is the campaign sometimes exciting or the election?

> *Clear:*   Now that the dreary campaign is finally over, the election starts today. It sometimes proves exciting.

Repetition

Eliminate any word that's been thoughtlessly used twice:

> *Careless:*   Marvin considered the opportunity of becoming the troop leader a valuable opportunity.
>
> *Improved*:   Marvin considered becoming the troop leader to be a valuable opportunity.

For advice on using *deliberate repetition*, see page 80.

Restrictive Clauses   See *Comma*, section 2.

Run-On Sentence (Fused Sentence)

Occasionally writers entirely forget to put in a period and run two sentences together, like this:

> Horace has a mangy dog without a brain in his head his name is Bowser.

Such a lapse is guaranteed to drive even the most patient readers to distraction. When you proofread, make sure that each sentence really *is* an acceptable sentence.

> Horace has a mangy dog without a brain in his head. His name is Bowser.

Those sentences are standard English, but a good writer would revise further to avoid wordiness:

> Horace has a mangy, brainless dog named Bowser.

Exercise   **8-13**

Put end punctuation where it belongs in the following items, and revise to avoid wordiness where necessary.

1 Playing blackjack is an absorbing hobby it might even absorb your bank account if you're not careful.
2 Blackjack is the only Las Vegas game in which the house does not have an overwhelming advantage in fact the players have an advantage if they use a system.
3 The best blackjack system involves remembering every card that has turned up the player keeps a running count of what cards are left in the deck and makes high or low bets accordingly.
4 The system is based on statistical tables compiled by computer expert Julian Braun of the IBM Corporation Braun does not play blackjack himself.
5 System players must be dedicated learning the system well takes 200 hours of memorization and practice.

Semicolon

1 The semicolon connects complete sentences that have closely related content:

> Clarence has three kittens; one of them is uncommonly homely.

> When angry, count four; when very angry, swear.

—Mark Twain

2   You should be sure to use a semicolon (instead of only a comma) when sentences are joined with a conjunctive adverb rather than with a coordinating conjunction: *and*, *but*, *or*, *for*, *nor*, *yet*, *so*. Here is a list of the most commonly used conjunctive adverbs:

accordingly	indeed	nonetheless
besides	instead	otherwise
consequently	likewise	then
furthermore	meanwhile	therefore
hence	moreover	thus
however	nevertheless	too

3   The type of connective you choose need not change the meaning, but it will change the punctuation. The following sentences, for instance, appear to require identical punctuation, but in standard usage the first requires a semicolon, the second only a comma:

> The demonstrators have a valid point; however, I can't condone their violence.

> The demonstrators have a valid point, but I can't condone their violence.

This rule may seem senseless, but there *is* a reason for the distinction. The conjunctive adverb is not a pure connective in the way the coordinating conjunction is. *However* in the first example can be picked up and moved to several other spots in the sentence as it suits your fancy. You could write:

> The demonstrators have a valid point; I can't, however, condone their violence.

or

> I can't condone their violence, however.

or even

> I, however, can't condone their violence.

You'll not be able to take such liberties with the coordinating conjunctions without producing nonsentences like these:

> I can't, but, condone their violence.

> I can't condone their violence, but.

> I, but, can't condone their violence.

It's easy to tell the difference between the pure conjunctions and the conjunctive adverbs if you've memorized the seven coordinating conjunctions: *and, but, or, for, nor, yet, so.* Other words likely to deceive you into thinking they are coordinating conjunctions are actually conjunctive adverbs.

4 Fortunately the problem of whether to use a comma *after* the adverb need no longer trouble you: it's optional now. Use a comma if you want to emphasize the adverb.

> The puppies are only three days old; however, you may pick one out without handling them.

> The puppies are only three days old; therefore you must not handle them.

NOTE: **The semicolon also substitutes for the comma in separating items in series when any of the items listed *already contains commas*, as in this sentence.**

> Moose-kitty tangled with an enormous, testy tomcat; triumphed momentarily; lowered his guard; then suffered a torn ear, a scratched eye, and mangled whiskers.

Sometimes the series may follow a colon:

> Clyde made several New Year's resolutions: to eat sensible, well-balanced meals; to study harder, sleep longer, and swear less; and to drink no more rum, tequila, or gin.

Exercise

Add semicolons to the following items where appropriate.

1 He believed that spicy foods were good for the heart, therefore, he ate jalapeña peppers for breakfast each morning.
2 He was tall, handsome, and rich, everyone loved him.
3 She divided her life into four distinct eras: blissful childhood, 1940–1954, carefree student life, 1954–1964, motherhood, 1964–1974, and finally, liberation, 1974 to the present.
4 He forgot to add oil, thus finding himself the victim of thrown rods and other incomprehensible malfunctions.
5 Seymour asked me to bring wine, preferably a rosé, baby Swiss cheese, and rolls, ideally fresh-baked, whole wheat ones, little did he know I'd already packed peanut butter sandwiches, strawberry Koolaid, and cheese curls.

Sentence Combining   See pages 58–60.

Shifts in Tense and Person   See also *Tense*, sections 1 to 3.

Sometimes your prose gets rolling along, and you shift into the wrong gear while you're moving, which results in an unpleasant grinding noise in your readers' heads. These shifts occur in tense and person.

1 *Don't shift tense without a reason.*

   a You may write in either present or past tense, depending upon how you approach your material. This sentence, for instance, is written in present tense:

   Bumper *is playing* poker.

Past tense would be:

   Bumper *was playing* poker.

   Bumper *had been playing* poker for five hours.

There's a good bit of variety within the two tenses, which there's no need to go into. The thing to remember is this: Choose either present or past tense and stay with it unless you have a reason to change. Here's an example of faulty tense switch:

> Bumper *was* intently *examining* his cards, when he *looks* up and *raised* the ante. Susie *yelps* and *gritted* her teeth but finally *throws* in her money.

You can, of course, switch tenses if you want to indicate a change occurring in time:

> Bumper *was raising* every bet for a while, but now he *is* simply *checking*.

Just be sure that you don't shift tenses without meaning to.

b   When you're writing about literature, be especially careful to avoid mixing past and present tense in your discussion of what happens in the book. It's traditional to describe literary happenings in the present tense (called the *historical* or *literary present*):

> Kingsley Amis's hero, Lucky Jim, *has* an imaginative humor that constantly *gets* him in trouble.

2   *Don't shift person, either.*   Shifting *person* (*I, you, she, they*) in a passage is a similar error. Here's an example of a triple whammy:

> *Faulty:*   As students, we learn the ghastly effects of procrastination. You find out that you just can't appreciate reading ten chapters of geography the night before a test. Most students know the grim thud in the gut that they feel when they stare at an exam and don't even understand the questions.

In that example the writer refers to the students in three different ways: *we* (first-person plural), *you* (second-person), and *they* (third-person plural). To revise the passage, stick to one pronoun:

> *Revised:*   As students, we learn the ghastly effects of procras-

tination. We find out that we just can't appreciate reading ten chapters of geography the night before a test. We become familiar with the grim thud in the gut that we feel when we stare at an exam and don't even understand the questions.

Spelling   See *Spelling Appendix*, pages 265 to 266.

If you get certain pairs of words confused, like *accept* and *except* or *affect* and *effect*, the "Glossary of Usage" beginning on page 237 will help you.

Split Infinitive

Current usage finds split infinitives perfectly acceptable:

> He tried *to* secretly *cause* fights between Chris and Ann.
>   *inf.*

Really is a common infinitive-splitter that can usually—quite beneficially—be left out of the sentence altogether.

> *Split:*   I began *to* really *appreciate* jug band music.
>   *inf.*

> *Improved:*   I began to appreciate jug band music.

A widely split infinitive can be awkward:

> *Widely split:*   He tried *to* purposely, secretly, and with malicious intent *cause* fights between Ann and Chris.

> *Improved:*   Purposely, secretly, and with malicious intent, he tried to *cause* fights between Ann and Chris.

Squinting Modifier

A *squinting modifier* is one that's ambiguous; it's placed between two words (or phrases) and could conceivably refer to either one of them:

Squinting: Marla thought <u>secretly</u> James ate too much.

Move the squinting modifier to a less confusing place in the sentence:

Clear: Marla *secretly* thought James ate too much.

Clear: Marla thought James *secretly* ate too much.

Subject   See *Agreement (Subject and Verb).*

Subjunctive Mood

Mood means the manner of expression of a verb. The verb forms you're most familiar with and use most often are in the indicative mood: I *cook*, you *eat*, he *washes* the dishes, they *sweep* the floor. Indicative mood is used for statements of fact. For statements and wishes contrary to fact (or highly unlikely) or for suppositions, many writers use *subjunctive* mood. You'll notice considerable difference in the verb forms for the *to be* verb but not so many for the regular verbs:

Indicative		Subjunctive	
I am	I was	I *be*	I *were*
he is	he was	he *be*	he *were*
you are	you were	you *be*	you were
they are	they were	they *be*	they were

Indicative	Subjunctive
I take	I take
he takes	he *take*
you take	you take
they take	they take

Remember Patrick Henry's "If this *be* treason"? And the phrase "if need be"? Those are examples of subjunctive mood. It used to be commonplace to use the subjunctive mood of all verbs, like, "If he *take* to his bed, he will surely expire." But now the subjunctive mood of the *to be* verb is practically the only one anyone worries about.

Although the subjunctive mood is no longer required in standard English, it's still expected by many people—especially in formal writing. Employing the subjunctive correctly will lend elegance to your writing and mark you as a well-educated user of the language.

1   Use subjunctive mood to express something that's contrary to fact, highly unlikely, doubtful, or speculative:

> If I were more refined, subjunctive mood would sound natural to me.

> Suppose he were confronted with an audience of subjunctive mood fanatics: he'd be in trouble if he were to use it incorrectly.

> He acts as though he were the smartest graduate of Podunk High, but he certainly doesn't know subjunctive mood.

2   Use subjunctive mood to express a strong necessity or a motion in a meeting:

> I move that all whale hunting be banned.

> It's crucial that you be present at this week's meeting.

Subordination   See pages 59 to 60.

Tense

Tense indicates time relationships. When you start trying to explain how it all works, you realize how amazing it is that most people do it right. Here are the basic tenses of English:

Present:	I walk.
Past:	I walked.
Future:	I will walk.
Present perfect:	I have walked.
Past perfect:	I had walked.
Future perfect:	I will have walked.

1   When you're writing about an event in present tense, it's natural to use past tense for past events and future for future events:

> I think that Hornsby wanted Clara to quit her job yesterday because he will not need as many clerks after the Christmas rush is over.

When you're writing about an event in past tense, you must use past perfect for events farther back in the past:

> Hornsby regretted that he had hired Clara for a permanent, full-time job.

2 The three perfect tenses (present perfect, past perfect, and future perfect) always show completed action:

> I have ridden the bus to campus for the past month.

> I had expected my Subaru to be fixed by last Monday.

> By the time I get my car back, I will have paid $215.39 just to get that windshield wiper fixed.

3 Sometimes the tense of a statement gets tricky when the surroundings of the statement are in past or future tense, but the statement itself is presently true or applicable:

> Clara realized last week that Hornsby is a greedy, manipulative phony.

Hornsby is still a greedy, manipulative phony, so the present tense is appropriate even though Clara figured him out a week ago.

> Jacob said that reading fiction is so pleasant it feels sinful.

Jacob said this in the past, but his statement about fiction still applies today, so the present tense is fine.

4 Every English verb has three principal parts that you need to know in order to form the tenses. Usually, the principal parts are just the present infinitive plus -*d*, -*ed*, or -*t*):

Present	Past	Past participle
walk	walked	(have, had) walked
dance	danced	(have, had) danced
spend	spent	(have, had) spent

But some verbs are *irregular;* that is, they form their past tense or past participle in odd ways. You just have to memorize the principal parts of these verbs. Here are twenty of the most common irregular verbs:

Present	Past	Past participle
am	was	been
begin	began	begun
break	broke	broken
burst	burst	burst (*not* busted)
choose	chose	chosen
come	came	come
do	did	done
drag	dragged	dragged (*not* drug)
drink	drank	drunk
forget	forgot	forgotten (*or* forgot)
go	went	gone
get	got	got (*or* gotten)
have	had	had
lay	laid	laid (meaning "placed")
lead	led	led
lie	lay	lain (meaning "reclined")
ride	rode	ridden
rise	rose	risen
run	ran	run
see	saw	seen
swim	swam	swum
take	took	taken
wake	waked (*or* woke)	waked (*or* woke)

Thesis Statement   See pages 10 to 12.

Title Tactics

Your title should tell your readers, as far as possible, what the paper is about.

1   Don't use a complete sentence but give more than a hint about your topic:

Useless: The Teacher and Research

Better: The Teacher and Research in Education

Good: Practical Research Ideas for Secondary Teachers

4   Luckily, he had remembered to actually bring his copy of *Paradise Lost* in case he had leisure reading time.

5   Hubert did feel badly because his roommate was not there to share the fun.

6   Sandra on the other hand did not arrive until a week after registration began.

7   She had only 3 paperback books with her.

8   She surprised her teachers by acting as though she was right on time.

9   Each of the books Sandra brought were special to her.

10 The books were Libra: Your Horoscope, Adventures of Huckleberry Finn, and Webster's New World Dictionary.

11 Although she didn't really believe in astrology Sandra found that reading over the list of Libra's good qualities cheered her up in times of depression.

12 *Huckleberry Finn* also cheered her up, supported her philosophy of life, and she never got bored no matter how many times she read it.

13 These characteristics of the novel were important to Sandra, for it meant that she never lacked a good book to read.

14 She sometimes forgot how to spell long words, therefore the dictionary was essential.

15 The dictionary was frequently used when she wrote papers.

16 It also helped her become drowsy when she'd drank too much coffee.

17 Huberts ability to spell was much better than most peoples.

18 His ability to dance, though, was lower than an elephant.

19 Sandra admired Hubert coming up with the correct spelling of *embarrass* every single time.

20 In her opinion, she had to admit that in the field of dancing, Hubert's Hustle was hopeless.

21 Sandra learned the Hustle at the New Age discotheque.

22 The surprising thing about some of Hubert's dance attempts, that include stumbles, jerks, and sometimes falls, do look quite fashionable sometimes.

23 Spelling, Hubert explained to Sandra, is a problem that can be cured only through memorization.

24 Dancing, Sandra explained to Hubert, becomes easy as pie with practice.

25 Hubert was eager to improve his dancing. Sandra wanted to become a better speller. They agreed to give each other lessons.

26 Hubert suggested, We could create a dance called the disco dictionary.

27 It's already created replied Sandra. I read about it in an article called Discomania in the New York Review of Books.

28 Walking into Sandra's room, Hubert's eye was caught by all the empty bookshelves.

29 He thought her lack of books was very strange he decided not to mention it, though.

30 She might still have her books packed up, he thought. Although it was the fifteenth week of the semester.

31 Sandra wasn't embarrassed by her empty bookshelves, in fact, she thought people often filled their shelves up just to impress others.

32 After supper on Tuesday, Sandra asked Hubert if he'd like to go to a lecture on how the *Oxford English Dictionary* was compiled in two hours.

33 She said that if students went to all the lectures that came up, you'd be busy every night of the week.

34 Hubert believed that people whose interests changed with every passing breeze were building on a foundation of jelly.

35 Sandra decided to go to the lecture while Hubert practices his Bump in front of the mirror.

Chapter 9

Glossary of Usage

This section describes the current usage of terms that are questionable as standard English (like the word *irregardless* and the use of *quotes* as a noun) and provides warnings about expressions that are nonstandard. It also explains the distinction between pairs of words that people often confuse (like *sit* and *set*, *lie* and *lay*, *effect* and *affect*). You will find, too, that quite a few formerly questionable expressions have recently become accepted as standard usage. (In order to refresh your memory about the characteristics of the various usage levels, see pages 71 to 74.) In making decisions on usage, I have been guided by Robert C. Pooley, *The Teaching of English Usage;* Roy H. Copperud, *American Usage: The Consensus;* Theodore Bernstein, *Dos and Don'ts and Maybes of English Usage;* several current collegiate dictionaries; and a stack of popular composition handbooks.

Usage simply means the way the language is used. But different people use the language in different ways. And even the same people use the language differently on different occasions. You probably speak more carefully in the classroom or on the job than you do when relaxing at the local pub. Good usage, then, is a matter of using language *appropriate* to the occasion. This chapter will tell you which expressions are appropriate for various occasions.

If you're in doubt about any terms that don't appear in this glossary, consult your trusty collegiate dictionary—but be sure it's of recent vintage. Even the best of dictionaries will be out of date on usage within ten years.

a/an

Use *a* before words beginning with consonant sounds; use *an* before words beginning with vowel sounds (*a, e, i, o, u*).

a martini	an Irish coffee
a tree toad	an armadillo
a hostile motorist	an hour exam (the *h* is silent)
a hopeful speech	an honest decision (the *h* is silent)
a one-car accident	an only child
(*o* sounds like *w*)	an historical event
a history text	

accept/except

Accept, a verb, means "to receive or to agree with."

We *accept* your excuse with reluctance.

Except as a preposition means "but or excluding."

Everyone's coming *except* Dinsdale.

Except as a verb isn't used much but means "to leave out."

The Dean agreed to *except* the foreign language requirement since I have lived in France.

advice/advise

When you *advise* someone, you are giving *advice*.

> *vb.*
> We *advise* you to stop smoking.

> *n.*
> Mavis refuses to follow our good *advice*.

affect/effect

The verb *affect* means "to influence." The noun *effect* means "the result of some influence."

> *n.*   *vb.*
> The *effect* on my lungs from smoking should *affect* my decision to quit.

> *vb.*
> Smoking adversely *affects* our health.

> *n.*
> LeRoy cultivates a seedy appearance for *effect*.

Just to confuse things further, *effect* can also be a verb meaning "to bring about." And *affect* can be a verb meaning "to cultivate an effect" or a noun meaning "emotional response."

> *vb.*
> We need to *effect* (bring about) some changes in the system.

> *vb.*
> Clyde *affects* (cultivates) a seedy appearance.

> *n.*
> Psychologists say that inappropriate *affect* (emotional response) is a feature of schizophrenia.

These last three meanings are seldom confused with the more widely used words above. Concentrate on getting those first, common meanings straight.

ain't

Still colloquial usage. Don't use it unless you're writing dialogue or trying to get a laugh.

all right/alright

Although *alright* is gaining acceptance in the world of advertising, you should stick with *all right* to be safe. *Alright* is definitely not *all right* with everybody yet.

almost/most

Don't write *most all;* standard usage still requires *almost all.*

> Jocasta ate *almost all* of the chocolate-covered cherries.

> Melvin sloshed down *most* of the eggnog.

a lot/alot

Even though *alike* is one word, *a lot* remains two.

already/all ready

Already means "before, previously, or so soon."

> Agnes has *already* downed two cheeseburgers.

All ready means prepared.

> Clarence is *all ready* to deliver his anti-junk food lecture.

altogether/all together

Altogether means "entirely, thoroughly."

> Clarence's analysis is *altogether* absurd.

All together means "as a group."

> Let's sing it *all together* from the top.

among/between

Use *among* when referring in general terms to more than two.

> Ashley found it difficult to choose from *among* so many delectable goodies.

Use *between* when referring to only two.

> She finally narrowed it down to a choice *between* the raspberry tart and the lemon meringue pie.

You can also use *between* when naming several persons or things individually.

> Seymour vacillates *between* the key lime pie, the Bavarian cream, and the baked Alaska.

analyzation

Don't use it. The word is *analysis*, and tacking on an extra syllable doesn't make it any grander.

anyways/anywheres

Nonstandard. Use *anyway* and *anywhere*.

apprise/appraise

To *apprise* means to "inform or serve notice."

> Marcella said the officer neglected to *apprise* her of her constitutional rights.

To *appraise* means to "evaluate or judge."

> Clarence *appraised* the situation carefully and caught the next plane for Venezuela.

as/like

Hardly anyone takes serious umbrage over the confusion of *as* and *like* anymore, but in formal writing, you should observe the distinction. *As* is a conjunction; hence it introduces clauses:

> This pie tastes good *as* everyone will agree.
>
> The other pie tastes *as if* he made it with artificial lemon.
>
> The good pie tastes *as though* he used real lemons.

Like is a preposition; thus it introduces phrases:

> The other pie tastes *like* artificial lemon.

author

Some people object to *author* as a verb, but the usage is becoming increasingly common.

> *Colloquial:*   Ann *authors* our monthly newsletter.
>
> *Formal:*   Ann *writes* our monthly newsletter.

awhile/a while

Written as one word, *awhile* is an adverb.

> Moose-cat frolicked *awhile* with Bowser.

A while is an article plus a noun.

> After *a while* Moose got bored and chased Bowser home.

bad/badly   See *Adjective/Adverb Confusion*, Chapter 8.

being as/being that

Don't use either one. Write *because* or *since*.

beside/besides

Don't use *beside* (at the side of) if you mean *besides* (in addition to).

> He leadeth me *beside* the still waters.

> Brandon has a math exam tomorrow *besides* his physics test.

between/among   See *among/between*.

center on/center around

As a matter of logic, you can't *center around* anything. Instead, you *center on* something.

choose/chose

Choose (rhymes with *ooze*) means a decision is being made right now.

> I find it hard to *choose* from a long menu.

Chose (rhymes with *toes*) means a choice has already been made.

> I finally *chose* the eggplant surprise.

compare/contrast

These words overlap in meaning. When you *contrast* two things, you are making a comparison. But as most instructors use the terms on examinations or in writing assignments, *compare* generally means to focus on similarities; *contrast* means to focus on differences.

Compare the music of the Beatles and the Rolling Stones.

Contrast the music of Lawrence Welk and Madonna.

complement/compliment

A *complement* is something that completes. The verb *to be* usually requires a *complement*.

Sheryl's purple scarf *complemented* her lavender sweater.

A *compliment* is a word of praise.

She got many *compliments* on her purple scarf.

continual/continuous

Careful writers will make a distinction. *Continual* means "repeatedly."

Bernard was *continually* late to class.

Continuous means "without interruption."

We suffered *continuous* freezing weather for almost three months.

could of/should of/would of

Nonstandard. Use *could have, should have, would have.*

Clyde *should have* (not *should of*) stopped at three beers.

deduce/infer/imply

Deduce and *infer* mean essentially the same thing—to reach a conclusion through reasoning.

Clarence *deduced* (or *inferred*) that Juanita was angry with him when she poured a pitcher of beer over his head.

But do not confuse these words with *imply*, which means "to state indirectly or hint."

> Juanita had *implied* several times earlier in the evening that she was displeased.

different from/different than

To be safe, stick with *different from* in formal writing.

> Gazelles are *different from* zebras in many ways.

You can save words, though, by introducing a clause with *different than;* this usage is now widely accepted.

Wordy:	Your aardvark looks *different from* the way I remembered.
Improved:	Your aardvark looks *different than* I remembered.

disinterested/uninterested

Although the distinction between these words is important, many people carelessly confuse them. *Disinterested* means "impartial."

> We need a totally *disinterested* person to judge the debate.

Uninterested means "not interested."

> Albert is totally *uninterested* in the moral tension of Renaissance drama.

dominant/dominate

Dominant is an adjective or a noun.

> George has a *dominant* personality.
> Brown eyes are genetically *dominant*.

Dominate is always a verb.

> Cecil's parents *dominate* him.

effect/affect   See *affect/effect.*

enthuse

Now acceptable in speech, but since the term still offends many people, avoid it in writing. Stick with *enthusiastic:*

Colloquial:	Brandon *enthuses* endlessly about the benefits of jogging.
Standard:	Brandon is endlessly *enthusiastic* about the benefits of jogging.

etc.

Don't use this abbreviation (meaning "and so on") unless you have a list in which the other examples are obvious (like large cities: Paris, London, Rome, etc.). Don't ever write *and etc.*; it's redundant.

everyday/every day

Use *everyday* as an adjective to modify a noun or pronoun.

> Gary is wearing his *everyday* jeans.

Use *every day* to mean "daily."

> It rains in the islands almost *every day.*

except/accept   See *accept/except.*

farther/further

Either word is acceptable to mean distance.

I can't walk a step *farther*, yet we have two miles *further* to go.

To indicate something additional, use *further*.

The judge would hear no *further* arguments.

former/latter

Unless you are a skillful writer, don't use these terms. Too often readers must look back in order to remember which was the former (the first mentioned) and which the latter (the last mentioned). For greater clarity, repeat the nouns.

fun

Do not use *fun* as an adjective in writing; use it as a noun.

Colloquial:	We had a *fun time* at the shore.
Standard:	We had *fun* at the shore.

good/well

Good is an adjective: it can be compared (*good, better, best*). *Well* can be an adverb (as in *Clyde writes well*) or an adjective (as in *Clarissa's kitty is well now*). What you want to avoid, then, is using *good* as an adverb.

Wrong:	Clyde writes *good*.
Right:	Clyde writes *well*.
Wrong:	Clarissa's job pays *good*.
Right:	Clarissa's job pays *well*.
Right:	I feel *good*.

Remember, though, that linking verbs take predicate adjectives, so you're right to say:

Clyde <u>looks</u> good.

Clarissa's attitude <u>is</u> good.

If you're in doubt, find a more precise expression:

> Clyde looks healthy (or happy or handsome).

> Clarissa's attitude is positive (or cooperative or hopeful).

> I feel frisky (or fine or great).

got/gotten

Both words are acceptable as past participles of the verb *to get*.

hanged/hung   See *hung/hanged*.

he or she/his or her

In order to include women in the language, many socially conscious people deliberately use *he or she* (instead of simply *he*) or *his or her* (instead of simply *his*, as grammarians decreed correct for over a century).[1] Equally as many people, though, still consider the double pronoun awkward, as indeed it can be if used ineptly, like this:

> *Awkward:*   The student must have his or her schedule signed by an adviser before he or she proceeds to pick up his or her class cards.

But that sentence can be easily revised to eliminate the excess pronouns.

> *Improved:*   The student must have his or her schedule signed by an adviser before picking up class cards.

Better yet, that sentence can be recast in the plural to eliminate the problem altogether.

---

[1] For an enlightening historical study explaining how the male bias in our language became so pronounced, see Julia P. Stanley, "Sexist Grammar," *College English*, 39 (March 1978), 800–811. Stanley contends, "The usage of *man, mankind,* and *he* in the early grammars of English was not generic in any sense of that term, however one might wish to construe it" (p. 801), and she supplies the evidence to prove her point.

Improved: Students must have their schedules signed by an
               adviser before picking up class cards.

You'll notice that the *idea* in the previous example was plural all along,
even though the first two versions were written in the singular. We are
taught early on to write singular even when we mean plural. We write
sentences like this:

A child should memorize *his* multiplication tables.

Really we mean *all* children should memorize *their* multiplication
tables. We need to kick that singular habit and cultivate the plural,
since our language has perfectly good nonsexist pronouns in the
plural—*they, their, them.*
     If you can't avoid using the singular—and sometimes you can't—
try to eliminate unnecessary pronouns.

Avoid: The winner should pick up *his* prize in person.

Better: The winner should pick up the prize in person.

If you can't eliminate the pronoun, an occasional *his or her*—or *her or
his*—is quite acceptable today.
     See also *man/person.*

hisself

Nonstandard. Don't use it unless writing dialect. Use *himself.*

hung/hanged

If you're talking about hanging pictures or hanging out clothes or just
letting it all hang out, the verb *hang* has these principle parts: *hang,
hung, hung, hanging.* But if you're referring to people hanging by the
neck, the verb goes *hang, hanged, hanged, hanging.*

Everyone felt that Melvin should have been *hanged*, drawn, and
quartered for forgetting the hot dogs.

imply/infer   See *deduce/infer/imply*

indefinite "you"   See *you* (*indefinite*).

in/into/in to

To be precise, use *in* to show location; use *into* to indicate motion.

> I was *in* the back seat when our car crashed *into* the train.

Often we use *in* not as a preposition (as in the previous example) but as an adverb functioning almost as part of a verb; *to go in*, *to sleep in*, *to give in*. With these fused verb-adverb constructions, keep *to* as a separate word.

> *adv.*
> Don't give *in* to pressure.
> *prep.*
> Don't play *into* their hands.

irregardless

Most people still steadfastly refuse to accept *irregardless* as standard English. Don't use it; say *regardless* or *nonetheless*.

is when/is where

Avoid both phrases, especially in writing definitions and instructions. Use *involves* or *occurs* instead.

> *Avoid:*   In tragedy, catharsis is when the audience feels purged of pity and fear.
>
> *Improved:*   In tragedy, catharsis involves purging pity and fear from the audience.

its/it's

Do not confuse these two terms. Memorize the two definitions if you have trouble with them, and when you proofread, check to be sure you haven't confused them accidently.

Its is a possessive pronoun.

> The dog chomped *its* own tail.

It's is a contraction of *it is* or *it has*.

> *It's* not an exceptionally smart dog.

> *It's* been impossible to train.

Perhaps it will help you keep these words straight if you remind yourself that none of the possessive pronouns has an apostrophe: *his*, *hers*, *ours*, *yours*, *theirs*, *its*. If you absolutely can't remember which is which, you should quit using the contraction: always write *it is*. Then, all you'll need to remember is *no apostrophe in* its.

kind of/sort of

Colloquial when used to mean *rather* or *somewhat*.

> *Colloquial:*   Moose is *sort of* snarly today.
>
> *Standard:*   Moose is *somewhat* touchy today.

The phrases can be used in standard English, but not as adverbs.

> *Standard:*   What *kind of* food will Moose-kitty eat?

Be careful, though, to avoid wordiness.

> *Wordy:*   Joe-kitty prefers a less fishy sort of food.
>
> *Improved:*   Joe-kitty prefers a less fishy food.

Never use *kind of a* or *sort of a* in writing.

> *Avoid:*   Moose is kind of a grouch today.
>
> *Improved:*   Moose is grouchy today.

latter/former   See *former/latter*.

lay/lie

To lay means to put or place; *to lie* means to recline. Be sure you know the principal parts; then decide which verb you need: to place—*lay, laid, laid, laying;* to recline—*lie, lay, lain, lying.* Remember that *lay* requires a direct object: you always *lay* something. But you never *lie* anything: you just *lie down,* or *lie quietly,* or *lie under a tree,* or *lie on a couch.* Notice the difference:

> *No object:*   Selma *lies* in the hammock.
>
> *Direct object:*   Selma *lays* her weary body in the hammock.

If you absolutely can't keep these verbs straight in your mind, choose another word.

> Selma *lounges* in the hammock.
>
> Selma *plops* her weary body in the hammock.

The verb *lie* meaning ''to tell a falsehood'' causes no problems since its principal parts are *lie, lied, lied, lying.* Hardly anyone past the age of five would say ''Selma *lied* down in the hammock.'' Similarly, the slang meaning of *lay* never confuses people. Nobody ever asks, ''Did you get *lain* last night?''

lead/led

Pronunciation causes the confusion here. *Lead* (rhymes with *bed*) means a heavy, grayish metal.

> Our airy hopes sank like *lead.*

Lead (rhymes with *seed*) is present tense of the verb meaning to guide.

> He *leads* me beside the still waters.

Led (rhymes with *bed*) is the past tense of the verb *lead.*

> LeRoy *led* the march last year, but he vows he will not *lead* it again.

leave/let

Standard usage allows either "*Leave* me alone" (meaning "go away")
or "*Let* me alone" (meaning "stop bothering me"). But since *let* really
means *to allow*, "*Leave* me give you some advice" is definitely
nonstandard. Use "*Let* me give you some advice before you *leave*."

lie/lay   See *lay/lie*.

like/as   See *as/like*.

lose/loose

Another problem in pronunciation and spelling. *Lose* (rhymes with
ooze) means to fail to keep something.

> If we *lose* [vb.] our right to protest, we will ultimately *lose* [vb.] our
> freedom.

Loose (rhymes with *goose*) means not tight.

> The noose is too *loose* [adj.] on your lasso.

man/person

The generic *man* (as the term is called) is supposed to include both
sexes—all human beings. But unfortunately the same word, *man*, also
means simply a male human being; thus the term is ambiguous.
Sometimes it includes both sexes; sometimes it doesn't—and sometimes
nobody can tell whether it does or doesn't. Also, *man* is another word,
like the generic *he*, that eclipses the female. To avoid this subtle
sexism, use *person* or *people* when you mean a person or people, not
just males.

> *Sexist:*   We want to hire the best *man* we can get for the job.
>
> *Fair:*   We want to hire the best *person* we can get for the job.

A number of compound words using the word *man* can be avoided with little difficulty.

Avoid	Prefer
chairman	chairperson, chair, moderator
congressman	representative, senator
councilman	council member
fireman	fire fighter
foreman	supervisor
mailman	mail carrier
mankind	humanity
manpower	work force
manmade	artificial, manufactured
policeman	police officer
salesman	salesperson

The tough one to replace is *manhole*. But did you ever stop to think that it could just as well be called a *sewer cover*?

See also *he or she/his or her*.

most/almost   See *almost/most*.

Ms.

Accepted by most and preferred by many, the term *Ms.* (rhymes with *whiz*) allows us to address women without indicating (or even knowing) their marital status, as the term *Mr.* has always done for men.

myself

Properly used, *myself* is either an intensive (I am going to fix the faucet *myself*) or a reflexive pronoun (I cut *myself* shaving). Do not use *myself* as a subject or an object in writing.

Colloquial:	Jocasta and *myself* are going to be partners.
Preferred:	Jocasta and *I* are going to be partners.
Colloquial:	Will you play tennis with Jocasta and *myself*?
Preferred:	Will you play tennis with Jocasta and *me*?

number/amount   See *amount/number*.

ones/one's

Use the apostrophe only with the possessive.

> To abandon one's friends is despicable.
>
> We were the first ones to report for duty.

prejudice/prejudiced

Although we seldom pronounce the *-ed*, do not leave it off in writing.

> *Prejudice* remains engrained in our society.
>
> Our society remains *prejudiced* against minorities.
>
> Almost everyone is *prejudiced* against something.
>
> Almost everyone harbors some sort of *prejudice*.

principal/principle

While we have numerous meanings for *principal*, the word *principle* basically means "rule": a person of high moral *principle*, a primary *principle* of physics. You can remember the *-le* spelling by association with the *-le* ending on *rule*. All other uses will end with *-al:* a high school *principal*, the *principal* on a loan, a *principal* cause or effect, the *principal* (main character) in a film or play.

quite/quiet

Be careful not to confuse these words. *Quite*, an adverb, means "entirely" or "truly." *Quiet* means the opposite of "loud." Do not confuse the two.

> Stanley was *quite* ready to yell, "*Quiet*, please!"

quotes

As a verb, *quotes* is standard English.

Leroy *quotes* Shakespeare even in bed.

But as a shortening of *quotation* or *quotation marks*, the term *quotes* is still considered colloquial by some people. This usage is presently changing, but for now, call them *quotations* in writing.

Avoid: You no longer need to put *quotes* around slang.

real/really

Don't use *real* as an adverb in writing.

Colloquial: Norman got into a *real* dangerous fight.

Standard: Norman got into a *really* dangerous fight.

But *really* (like *very*) is a limp, overworked word. Either leave it out or find a more emphatic word.

Improved: Norman got into a dangerous fight.

Norman got into an incredibly dangerous fight.

reason is because

This phrase causes faulty predication. Use instead, ''The reason is that . . . ,'' or rephrase your sentence.

Avoid: The reason we are swamped with trash is because I forgot to put the garbage out.

Better: The reason we are swamped with trash is that I forgot to put the garbage out.

Better: We are swamped with trash because I forgot to put the garbage out.

rise/raise

You never *rise* anything, but you always *raise* something. Prices *rise*, spirits *rise*, curtains *rise*, but you *raise* cain, or *raise* corn, or *raise* prices.

Taxes are *rising* because Congress has *raised* the social security withholding again.

If you can't keep these verbs straight, avoid them.

Taxes are going up.

Congress keeps increasing taxes.

she or he See *he or she/she or he*.

should of See *could of/should of/would of*.

sit/set

You don't *sit* anything and you always *set* something (with these exceptions, which are seldom confused: the sun *sets*, jello and concrete *set*, hens *set*). We *sit* down or we *sit* a spell; we *set* a glass down or we *set* a time or we *set* the table. But for some inexplicable reason, we say in standard English, "The principal *sat* Herman down and gave him a stern lecture." If anyone can figure that one out, please let me know.

sort of/kind of   See *kind of/sort of*.

split infinitives

Go right ahead and split your infinitives if you feel like it, but don't rend them asunder. A single adverb between *to* and the verb is now acceptable (*to* hastily *plan* a party), but several intervening words are usually considered awkward.

supposed to/used to

Since we never hear the *-d* sound in these phrases when we talk, the *-d* is easy to forget in writing. Whenever you write either term, be sure to add the *-d*.

than/then   See *then/than*.

their/there/they're

Do not confuse these words. *Their* is a possessive adjective or pronoun.

> *Their* dog is friendly. That dog is *theirs*.

There is an adverb or an expletive.

> *There* she goes. *There* is no problem.

They're is a contraction of *they are*.

> *They're* gone.

If you have trouble spelling *their*, remember that all three—*the*ir, *the*re, and *they*'re—start with *the-*.

theirselves

Don't use it unless writing dialect. The accepted term is *themselves*.

then/than

These words have quite different meanings. *Then* usually suggests a time.

> First we'll pick up the ice; *then* we'll get the pop.

Than usually suggests a comparison.

> No one drinks cola faster *than* Seymour.

thusly

Don't use it except for humor; write simply *thus*.

to/too/two

To is usually a preposition, sometimes an adverb, and also introduces an infinitive.

> *to* the depths, push the door *to*, *to* swing

Too is an adverb.

> *Too* much noise.
>
> Selma is going *too*.

Two is the number.

> *two* hedgehogs, *two* bricks

try and/try to

Although we frequently say, "I'm going to *try and* get this job done," the usage is still informal. In formal writing, stick with *try to*.

uninterested/disinterested   See *disinterested/uninterested*.

used to/supposed to   See *supposed to/used to*.

very

Avoid this colorless, exhausted word. Find one more exact and expressive (extremely, considerably, fully, entirely, completely, utterly) or just leave it out. See also *real/really*.

weather/whether

Do not confuse these words. *Weather* is what goes on outside. *Whether* introduces an alternative.

> I can't decide *whether* the *weather* will be suitable for a picnic.

who/which/that

Use *who* to refer to people (or animals you're personifying).

> The person *who* lost three keys . . .
>
> Lenin, *who* is Susie's cat, . . .

Use *which* to refer to animals or nonliving things.

> The earth *which* blooms in spring . . .
>
> The cat *which* lives at Susie's . . .

Use *that* to refer either to people or things.

> The person *that* lost these keys . . .
>
> The earth *that* blooms in spring . . .
>
> The cat *that* lives at Susie's . . .

If you're in doubt about whether to use *who* or *whom*, see *Case of Pronouns*, section 5, in Chapter 8.

whose/who's

Whose is the possessive pronoun or adjective.

> *Whose* alligator is that? Find out *whose* alligator that is.

Who's is the contraction of *who is*.

> *Who's* going to dispose of that alligator?

would of   See *could of/should of/would of*.

you (indefinite)

In informal writing, you may always address your readers as *you* (as I have done in this sentence). Somewhat questionable, though, is the use of *you* to mean just anyone (the *indefinite you*).

In France if *you* buy a loaf of bread, *you* get it without a wrapper.

If you're writing on a formal level, you should use the third-person singular *one*.

In France if *one* buys a loaf of bread, *one* gets it without a wrapper.

your/you're

Your is a possessive adjective or pronoun.

The porpoise is *your* problem; the porpoise is *yours*.

You're is a contraction of *you are*.

Let me know when *you're* leaving.

Exercise on Words Frequently Confused   **9-1**

The following sentences contain words that sound alike but mean different things, like *quite/quiet*, *its/it's*, and *sit/set*. In each sentence, choose the appropriate term from the words in parentheses.

1 I have been (lead/led) astray again.
2 Lenin is even plumper (then/than) Spiny Norman.
3 (Its/It's) not the money; (its/it's) the (principal/principle) of the thing.
4 Those most in need of (advice/advise) seldom welcome it.
5 Clyde can't study if his room is (to/too) (quiet/quite).
6 The automobile is a (principal/principle) offender in contributing to air pollution.
7 Our spirits (rose/raised) with the sun.
8 They had a frisky time when (there/their) goose got (lose/loose).
9 Let's (lie/lay) down and talk this over.
10 That (continual/continuous) drip from the faucet is driving me to drink.
11 You ought to (appraise/apprise) the situation carefully before you decide (weather/whether) to file a complaint.
12 (You're/Your) decision could (affect/effect) your career.
13 If you (choose/chose) to file, you should not harbor the illusion that all (you're/your) problems will be solved.
14 Why don't we (sit/set) this one out?

15 (Your/You're) going to be sent to Outer Mongolia if you (accept/except) this job.
16 Clyde tends to (dominant/dominate) the conversation with his (continual/continuous) complaints about the IRS.
17 I could (infer/imply) from his complaints that he owes back taxes.
18 If the (weather/whether) improves, (then/than) we will plant the garden.
19 Any news program will usually (appraise/apprise) you of a late frost.
20 Snow peas will not be (affected/effected) by a light frost.
21 I (advice/advise) you to pick them young.
22 The administration has (lain/laid) down firm (principles/principals) concerning campus dissent.
23 I (chose/choose) strawberry last time, and it was all right, (accept/except) there weren't any strawberries in it.
24 Clyde was (quiet/quite) outraged.
25 How did that dog (lose/loose) (its/it's) tail?
26 Many men mistakenly think (their/they're) supposed to be the (dominant/dominate) sex.

Exercise on Assorted Matters of Usage   9-2

Most of the sentences below contain examples of questionable usage. Revise those sentences that need changing in order to be acceptable as standard English. Some contain multiple mistakes.

1 Stanley and myself moved in a new apartment.
2 We need to quickly, thoroughly, and painstakingly perform the analyzation of that substance again.
3 Did Clyde author that report all by hisself?
4 Having been raised on a farm, Henrietta is disinterested in urban entertainments.
5 Seymour baked alot of cookies.
6 You could of busted the lawnmower on that huge rock.
7 For once, try and do what you're supposed to.
8 Hopefully, we are already to go now.
9 I'm going to put quotes around this slang, irregardless of what the book says.
10 Most everyone which is liable to come has all ready got here.
11 A banquet is where you eat alot of food and can't help but be bored by the speeches.
12 If we go altogether, we should be alright.
13 A person may buy his or her ticket from his or her union representative.

14 You would of had less problems if you would of centered around the main issue better.

15 The real reason I'm not coming is because I'm not interested anyways.

16 My ideas are all together different than those of the speaker.

17 If you live in Rome, you should do like the Romans do.

18 Clyde and Claudia got theirselves involved in a accident all ready on their new motorcycle.

19 Clyde use to enthuse about the virtues of being safety conscious.

20 Now his safety record ain't any different from anybody else's.

21 If you turn the key, thusly, the engine will start.

22 Where is the monkey wrench at?

23 If I'd known you were coming, I would of left.

24 Seymour used to scrub the bathtub every day.

25 Being as you promised, you must come, irregardless of the inconvenience.

26 Clarence is headed for the hospital, as he hurt hisself hunting.

Spelling Suggestions

For a time people were considerably more relaxed about correct spelling than we are today. William Shakespeare, demonstrating his boundless creativity, spelled his own last name at least three different ways. John Donne wrote "sun," "sonne," or "sunne," just as it struck his fancy. But along about the eighteenth century, Dr. Samuel Johnson decided things were out of hand. He took it upon himself to establish a standard for the less learned and brought out his famous dictionary. The language has refused to hold still, even for the stern-minded Dr. Johnson, but some folks have been trying to tame it ever since.

Today educated people are expected to be able to spell according to the accepted standard. Nobody encourages a lot of creativity in this area. So if you didn't learn to spell somewhere back in grade school, you've got a problem. At any bookstore you'll find an abundance of pamphlets that promise to place you among the ranks of superlative spellers. But these are seldom helpful. Anybody who memorizes well enough to remember all those rules plus all those exceptions probably knows how to spell already.

TRY LISTING

My advice is to keep a list of all the words you *know* you misspell. Start now. Add to it whenever you discover you've misspelled a word. If you keep adding the same word—especially an easy, often-used word, like "writing" or "coming"—make a point of *remembering* that you can't spell it so that you can look it up. And keep your dictionary handy when you write.

TRY DODGING

Sometimes you can switch to another word when you realize you don't know how to spell the one you had in mind. It's tough with little everyday words, but use your ingenuity if you can't use your dictionary. Suppose you want to say, "I have trouble with writing," and you can't remember whether "writing" has one or two *t*'s. Rather than risk a serious spelling error (and the more common the word, the more serious the error), scratch that out and say, "I don't write as well as I'd like to."

TRY PROOFREADING

Spelling is intimately tied up with proofreading. A quick read-through won't catch careless spelling errors, and it won't make you stop and look up words that just don't look right the way you wrote them. It will do you no good to shrug and say, "Oh, I'm a terrible speller," as though it were the same as "Oh, I'm a hemophiliac." If you know you're a sorry speller, don't worry about it on the rough draft: that could cramp your style. But do look up all words you're uncertain about before you type the final copy, and correct misspellings that you discover when you proofread.

Should you be so fortunate as to have a friend or relative who can spell, you are among the blessed. Beg or bribe this gifted person to check your papers for misspelled words. And don't forget to add these words to your list after you correct them.

Writing Job Application Letters and Résumés

Whether you go into business as a career or not, you'll eventually need to write at least one extremely important business letter: a job application, accompanied by a résumé listing your qualifications. You will find here a sample of each to use as models.

TIPS FOR WRITING

When you do your letter, adopt a polite tone and be brief. Your résumé will include most of the pertinent information. Organize before you write. If possible, try to focus your remarks on what you can do for the person you're writing to, rather than the reverse. Be sure to make a rough draft and revise it until it sounds perfect. Get your friends and loved ones to rally round and offer suggestions for improvement. Check your spelling and punctuation carefully.

TIPS FOR TYPING

In typing the final copy, follow the format of the model closely. Originality is not appreciated in business correspondence. Use the best paper you can afford, and be sure the final version looks handsome—evenly spaced on the page with no more than a couple of inconspicuous corrections.

Your résumé may be duplicated commercially after you've typed it once, but each letter must be retyped individually. Don't forget to proofread—at least twice.

Exercise

Go through the help wanted ads of your local newspaper and choose a job that sounds like one you might like. Write a letter of application and a résumé. Don't mail them unless you want the job, but don't throw them away either. You can use the letter as a guide when you write the real thing. And you'll only need to update the résumé.

500 West Main Street
Normal, IL 61761
March 15, 1988

Ms. Marna Winters
Personnel Manager
Great Western Publishing Corp.
7777 State Street, Room 456
Chicago, IL 60606

Dear Ms. Winters:

Effective opening →

Do you need a good, experienced proofreader or copy editor?

Presenting qualifications {

For two summers I worked as a proofreader at The Daily Deluge in Colfax, Illinois, and for three years as a part-time advertising copywriter for radio station WXYZ in Normal. As the enclosed résumé indicates, I majored in English and minored in journalism at Illinois State University.

Summarizing experience {

My experience with various writing and proofreading assignments should prove useful to your firm. I know a position with your nationally known organization would be satisfying to me, as it would further my professional goal of becoming an editor.

Setting up interview →

May I come in for an interview at your convenience? Thank you for your consideration.

Sincerely,

Sue LeSeure

Enclosure: Résumé

Figure B-1: Sample Job Application Letter

Sue LeSeure
500 W. Main St.
Normal, IL 61761
Telephone: 309/452-9999

Experience

Oct. 1986 to present (during school term)	Station WXYZ, Normal, IL Part-time, 20 hours per week. Wrote advertising copy and solicited ads.
June-August 1987 June-August 1986	The Daily Deluge, Colfax, IL Full-time proofreader (substituted for head proofreader, 1987).
June-August 1985	Gilbey's Variety Store, Colfax, IL Sales clerk (with stocking and pricing duties). Also made deliveries and called in supply orders.

Education

Sept. 1985-June 1988	Illinois State University Will receive B.A. in English, June 1988.
Sept. 1984-June 1985	Baskerville Community College
Sept. 1980-June 1984	Octavia High School
Scholastic honors:	Earned a 3.46 grade point average (on a 4.0 scale). George Canning Scholarship in English Literature, 1987-88. Illinois State Scholarship, 1984-1988.
Technical training:	Attended a two-week seminar on ''Advertising in Today's Marketplace,'' sponsored by College of Business and McLean County Association of Commerce and Industry.

Personal Data

Age:	24	Married, no children
Health:	Excellent	Willing to relocate
Memberships:	Student Association for Women; Journalism Club (President, 1986-87)	
Hobbies:	Photography, swimming	

References

Ms. Mary Gilbey, Manager Gilbey's Variety Store 555 S. Fifth Street Colfax, IL 61763 Phone: 309/723-9999	Dr. Charles Harris Prof. of English Illinois State University Normal, IL 61761 Phone: 309/436-9999	Mr. Waldo Withersnorp Advertising Manager Radio Station WXYZ 112 Beaufort Avenue Normal, IL 61761

Figure B-2:   Sample Résumé

Acknowledgments

Maya Angelou, excerpt from *I Know Why the Caged Bird Sings*, 1969. Reprinted by permission of the publisher, Random House, Inc.

James Baldwin, excerpt from *Nobody Knows My Name*, 1959. Reprinted by permission of Doubleday, a division of Bantam, Doubleday, Dell Publishing Group, Inc.

Stephen Brill, excerpt from "The Traffic (Legal and Illegal) in Guns," *Harper's*, September 1979. Copyright © 1977 by Stephen Brill. Reprinted by permission of Sterling Lord Literistic, Inc.

Richard Champlin, M.D., excerpt from "With the Chernobyl Victims," *Los Angeles Times*, July 6, 1986. © Richard Champlin. Reprinted by permission.

Joan Didion, excerpt from "In Bed," *The White Album*, Washington Square Press, 1979. Copyright © 1979 by Joan Didion. Reprinted by permission of Simon and Schuster, Inc.

Annie Dillard, excerpt from "Innocence in the Galapagos," *Harper's*, May 1975. © by *Harper's* magazine. Reprinted by special permission.

Richard Flint, excerpt from "Corn of a Different Color," *Rodale's Organic Gardening*, November 1982. Copyright 1982 Rodale Press, Inc., USA. All rights reserved. Reprinted by permission.

Harper's, excerpt from "Wraparound," April 1975. © by *Harper's* magazine.
Reprinted by special permission.

Mark Kane, excerpt from "The Tomato: Still Champion," *Rodale's Organic
Gardening*, March 1982. Copyright 1982 by Rodale Press, Inc., USA.
All rights reserved. Reprinted by permission.

Philip Langdon, excerpt from "Burgers! Shakes!" *The Atlantic Monthly*,
December 1985. © Philip Langdon 1985. Reprinted by permission of
Philip Langdon.

Ogden Nash, excerpt from "Reflections on Ice-Breaking," from *Verses from
1929 On*. Copyright © 1930 by Ogden Nash. Reprinted by permission
of Little, Brown and Company, Publishers.

Newsweek, excerpt from "Say It's Really So, Joe!" *Newsweek*, June 2, 1975,
and from "The Smell of Death," *Newsweek*, February 1, 1971.
Copyright 1975, 1971 by Newsweek Inc. All rights reserved. Reprinted
by permission.

A. B. Paine, excerpt from *Mark Twain: A Biography*. Harper, 1912. Reprinted
by permission of Harper & Row, Publishers.

Robert C. Pooley, excerpt from *The Teaching of English Usage*, 2d ed.
Copyright © 1946, 1974 by the National Council of Teachers of English.
Reprinted by permission.

Katherine Anne Porter, excerpt from "The Never Ending Wrong," *The
Atlantic Monthly*, June 1977. © 1977 by Katherine Anne Porter.
Reprinted by permission.

Psychology Today, excerpt from "Newsline: Sexuality—Misreading the
Signals," *Psychology Today*, October 1980. Copyright © 1980.
Reprinted by permission.

Anne Sexton, excerpt from "From Eleanor Boylan Talking with God," *All
My Pretty Ones*, 1962. © 1962 by Anne Sexton. Reprinted by permission
of Houghton Mifflin Co.

Mary V. Taylor, excerpt from "The Folklore of Usage," *College English*,
April 1974. Copyright © 1974 by the National Council of Teachers of
English. Reprinted by permission.

Mark Twain, excerpt from *Mark Twain's Autobiography*. © 1924 by Clara
Gabrilowitsch. Reprinted by permission of Harper & Row, Publishers.

Liv Ullmann, excerpt from *Changing*. Reprinted by permission of the
publisher, Random House, Inc.

Gore Vidal, "The State of the Union," *Matters of Fact and Fiction: Essays
1973–1976*. First appeared in *Esquire*, May 1975. Copyright © 1975 by
Gore Vidal. Reprinted by permission of The William Morris Agency on
behalf of the author.

Index